999 Powerful Affirmations for Black Women:

Daily Affirmations to Hack your Mind to Positivity, Confidence, Health, Money, Success & Motivation. Learn to Overcome Anxiety and Depression in Modern World.

About The Book…………………………………………...6

INTRODUCTION…………………………………9

The Beginning Before The Chapters………………19

Affirmations For The Black Woman Who Is Just Starting In Business……………………………46

Chapter Two………………………………………...55

Chapter Three……………………………………71

Chapter Four………………………………………88

Chapter Five………………………………………110

Chapter Six………………………………………139

Chapter Seven………………………………………158

Chapter Nine……………………………………219

Chapter Ten………………………………………241

Chapter Eleven……………………………………263

Chapter Twelve………………………………286

Chapter Thirteen………………………………305

Chapter Fourteen………………………………320

Conclusion……………………………………334

About The Book

Have you ever imagined what your life would look like if you didn't entertain any form of negative talk around you? It would be fantastic. It is one of the most beautiful things ever. You might raise your eyebrows in surprise and ask me if I am not aware that negative talking and self-sabotaging are inherent behaviours among people. I am very much aware of this, but you can eliminate all of that in your own space. You shouldn't let the norms and the things everyone else does dictate how you should live your life. You can reprogram your mind and create the life you want for yourself. It is no stroll in the park, but it is possible, and I know that you can do it. Yes, you can do it even if you do not know how to do it. You know, experts were once novices. This book exists to teach you how to reprogram your life into the life you desire. Read on and watch me unravel it all to you.

It is not unusual to find people who talk down on themselves simply because things are not going as they should for them. This behaviour can make such people blind to the magic in themselves. Each and every one of us has our magic and wonder. But you tell me, how can you see the magic in you when you blind yourself with negative talk and self-pity? How do you expect to get that job when all you do is rant on and on about how much you don't deserve it? What makes you think you are less qualified because you are a black woman? Why do you think you're not beautiful enough because you are not the standard the world is used to?

You may not realise the power of the words you speak to yourself until you sit and carefully analyze how much negativity has cost you and how powerful a single word could be. If you've been living a life of negativity to this point, I'm going to help you stop. Negativity is no thriving ground. Believe me, it is one of the worst places to be in. You should know this one truth; negativity has no advantage. Rather, it diminishes you continuously until you become one of the things you have always dreaded and hoped not to become. I know you don't want to walk that road at all. So, I'll help you attain great heights by exploring positivity and affirmations step by step.

999 Powerful Affirmations for Black Women will help you take all the big steps you need and help you live and create your ideal life through powerful words and speaking all that you want into your life. This book also has key points for every section. These key points are a summary of the section. Even if you're too busy to read the book word by word, you can go directly to the key points and get value from them. This book is written to serve you to the fullest. Get this book today and begin your journey into reprogramming your mind and becoming the badass Queen that you are meant to be. It is time to explore all of your magic. Shall we begin?

INTRODUCTION

It's the repetition of affirmations that leads to beliefs. And once that belief becomes a deep conviction, things begin to happen.
—Muhammad Ali.

The first time I saw the quote above, it didn't make any sense to me. I wondered how things would begin to happen just because someone repeated a string of positive words. No matter how I tried to make sense out of it, it still sounded crazy to me. It was absurd. I only began to understand affirmations better when I began to associate with them deeply. Affirmations are way beyond saying 'today is a good day when you get up from bed in the morning. It is a thing of the heart and soul. It requires that you pour yourself into it without holding back anything at all. Affirmation is a lot of soul and inner energy and belief. That's why it requires consistency too.

I know you're getting curious here. Questions are brewing in your mind already, aren't they? Come along with me. I'll take you through what you need to know about affirmations. So, the first question is; what is an affirmation? It's a very simple answer. An affirmation is simply a positive, encouraging, strengthening and powerful statement that one makes to eliminate negative thoughts and fear. It's simply amazing, right? Yes, this simplicity is so powerful that it can turn your life around forever. It is a gradual but steady process.

First, you must understand that affirmation is not magic. You don't begin an affirmation today and expect it to work the very next moment. It is a process. There is no set time frame within which affirmations work. Rather, they work on their own volition. But I have come to learn that the greater my belief in my affirmations, the faster they all manifest. You gradually become the things you affirm. You have the rare ability to become anything that you speak into your being. Be it positivity or negativity. So, you make the choice. Would you choose negative talk or positive talk? The choice lies on you, but I encourage you to choose positivity. That's what this book is all about!

I remember calling affirmations bluff because I couldn't just fathom the working principles behind them. I mean, how could things become better because I said they would? I kept on doubting the power of affirmations until I came across an affirmation theory by Claude Steele which made me understand that affirmations work first by reworking the mind. It would take a negative mind a lot of work to actually experience the power of affirmations. This is because negativity has a way of blinding a person to the good things. Do you remember that one person who always made you feel like you were not doing enough no matter how much you tried? You'd feel as though you were the worst person on earth. You'd feel yourself crumbling from the inside. It is a very terrible way to feel. I know this first hand because I have had my own share of it in the past. If negative talk can get into one so much and make one feel very terrible, don't you think positive talk can also get to one and reshape things? I believe you get the drift now! This is how it works. Descartes the philosopher wasn't joking at all when he said 'I think, therefore I am'.

When you think of yourself as something and affirm that thing to yourself very often, it stays in your subconscious. At that level, your whole being would be convinced of that thing. You'll begin to manifest that thing.

I'll give you an example. I used to have this potted plant that I used in designing my home. When the gardener brought in this plant, it was very green and beautiful. It looked very tender and frail too. I appreciated the beauty of the plant and asked the gardener if the plant would last considering the fact that it looked really tender. You know what he told me?

He said 'it'll last as long as you nurture it'. His answer amazed me for a while. I wondered what he really meant by that answer.

Every morning, I'd grumble while watering the plant because I expected it to die soon. I'd say 'Hey pretty one, I'll water you anyway. But I know you'll die soon…'

Then, the plant began to wither and die. This happened within a very short time! When I noticed it, I concluded that my prediction was right after all.

I was like, 'I saw it coming all along! I knew you wouldn't make it far'. I called my gardener to let him know about the plant and he told me I fed the plant a lot of negativity. That it was only manifesting what I wished for. Boy, did that amuse me! A plant would die just because I said so! Tell me another tale, please.

I decided to 'nurture' the plant back to life by speaking good things to it while I watered every morning. I'd water and say 'my beautiful plant, look how you dazzled me today. See how green you are. So full of life and color. I love you, my plant...' this sounds weird to you, doesn't it? I'd have found it weird too if I didn't have this experience. After some time, my plant began to bounce back to life. It was like magic. It surprises me to this day. It was as though the plant could hear every single affirmation I made in its favour every morning. It was then I realized the power of positive affirmations and how they could affect everything around me in a good way.

Does my little encounter with my plant amaze you? You'll get further amazements in this book which is written for your gorgeous and amazing self. I understand the struggles black women go through each day in their quest to better their worlds and leave their own marks in the world. It's overwhelming sometimes, very much overwhelming. So I won't let you go through all of the stressful journeys alone. This affirmation book is written for you to strengthen you on days you feel like giving it all up, to speak peace and love and positivity into your life on days the fights within self threaten to overpower you, to share in your joys, to make you have more and more control over your life. You are the boss babe. Boss babes are in control of everything that concerns them.

Some people find it difficult to be consistent with making affirmations. If you are this kind of person, you don't have to be worried one bit. I have solutions for you. First of all, you must understand that every single thing is a process. It's just like the growth of children. Today, you see them crawling. Tomorrow you see them trying to stand on their own. Of course, they go through so many falls while at it. But that doesn't stop them from attaining balance because they'd eventually learn how to walk and run and even jump! That, my friend, is the beauty of the process. You walk despite the falls.

So, gorgeous black woman, believe me when I say it's okay that you don't know exactly how to go about this affirmation thingy. I've been in that place before. Now, I literally can't live without affirmations. I can't imagine starting my day without speaking positivity, power and strength into it first. Isn't this very surprising for someone who once said affirmations were empty talks? So, come with me. We'll go through your affirmation journey together. I am holding your hand through these pages on every step. There's no need to fret about a thing. I've got you! With this book, you'll get to know the power of affirmations in all its forms. You'll also enjoy the luxury of creating the kind of life that you have always dreamed of by speaking it into your life. Don't you think it is high time you let go of all the negativity that society, environment, toxic people and others once made you embrace?

It is high time you shaped your space into your kind of life. Queens like you don't thrive in toxic spaces. I'll walk with you as you step out of those toxic spaces with self-affirmations. It's not a very easy journey, but trust me, it will be worth the while. Let us begin. But before we begin, I'd first answer that one question that many people have asked and still wonder about. When is the best time to say affirmations?

When Is The Best Time To Say Affirmations?

A lot of people have made different rules about the best time to say affirmations. The truth is; there are no rules to it. You can speak power into yourself and your whole existence at any time of the day and you would still get brilliant results.

Some people argue that morning is the best time for it. You know, the first thing you do after waking up from sleep. Making so many rules for affirmations could make it boring and difficult for you. So, it all lies on you to choose the most suitable time for you and stick to it. You could do it in the morning when you wake up, you could also do it in between the day while you go about your activities. Either of these are fine. But we advise you to try saying your affirmations in the morning before you get engrossed in the activities of the day. You know, once that happens, you may not get the time and concentration you need to say your affirmations the way you want to say them. Concentration is very vital in the making of good affirmations. Remember this always.

Now all you have to do is proceed with me to the next chapter as I welcome you into the world of life changing, powerful and beautiful affirmations.

The Beginning Before The Chapters.

Everyday's a chance to begin again. Don't focus on the failures of yesterday, start today with positive thoughts and expectations.
—Catherine Pulsifer

The title of this part of the book sounds really crazy, right? Well, a little fun would do a black woman no harm. So, this part of the book is some sort of mini section before the main chapters. Say, it is a sort of preamble to what you would get in the book.

I am dedicating this section to you and your day. The beginning of your days especially. You know, the beginning of a thing is the most important and most delicate part of it. It is for this reason that I'm writing this section sweetly and delicately just for you. There's something that I have noticed about myself. I don't know if it's that way with other people. How I begin my day plays a very crucial role in how it turns out. For instance, if I begin my day with a lot of negative energy and the acceptance of things that I do not want, it tends to affect the rest of my day. When I realized that, I began to take the beginnings much more seriously. Instead of gloating over my bulky workload first thing in the morning, I'd rather speak power and strength into my day. I'd speak these heart-felt and beautiful words of affirmation, bless my day and decree it a blessing.

I've been doing this for so long now that it has become an essential part of my routine. It is not just routine now, it is a habit. A very powerful one at that. I know you want to experience this kind of power too. I am ready and beyond willing to lead you into it. It is for this reason that I'll begin these affirmations. Now, hold my hand and journey with me through some delicate, warm and power-filled affirmations curated specially for the beginnings.

Affirmations for The Beginning

1. I declare my day a blessing.
2. Today, I choose joy and laughter. I'll laugh loudly and be joyful until the end.
3. I excel beyond doubts today.
4. I am in control of my day.
5. I'll not let anything steal my joy nor rob me of my peace.
6. I shine brilliantly like the sun.
7. Today is my day of rising, and I'll rise with so much elegance that the sun would become jealous of me.
8. I thrive in all areas of my life.
9. My day is full of excellence and unparalleled success.
10. I thrive everywhere.
11. I blossom like the morning sun.
12. I step away from every distraction that would ruin my day.
13. I perform beyond my expectations today.
14. Today, I choose myself.
15. I am a very beautiful work in progress.
16. I attract positivity today.

17. I know no bleakness today.

18. I am courageous enough to move away from the things that no longer serve me.

19. I start my day with joy and end with joy.

20. I connect with people who are instrumental to the achievement of my goals.

21. I dream big dreams today and they come to pass.

22. I do not struggle today.

23. I stand out with ease and elegance.

24. I live my biggest dreams.

25. I sing my best songs in the most sonorous of voices.

26. I am loved fully.

27. I am not overwhelmed by the activities of the day.

28. I have enough strength to help me get through my day.

29. I rid my day of stagnation.

30. I move forward in ease.

31. I reach my destinations safely.

32. I do not get into embarrassing situations.

33. I work with my head held high.

34. I do not cower to defeat.

35. I rise above obstacles.

36. I thrive in every place.

37. I am blessed in big measures.

38. I take advantage of opportunities.

39. I create my happiness.

40. I am aware of myself and the power I possess.

41. I give no one the power to toss me about.

42. I am fully in control of my life and that concerts me.

43. I am aware that I am more than enough.

44. I show myself as much care as I need.

45. I am independent and whole.

46. I do not stay in places that shrink me.

47. I have value to offer.

48. I'm so valuable that mediocrity hides at the sight of me.

49. I speak boldly and wisely.

50. I stand up for myself when the need arises.

51. I do not keep mum in uncomfortable situations.

52. My mental health is safe and healthy.

53. I am a big body of blessings.

54. My life is full of ease.

55. I know no difficulty.

56. I shine effortlessly.

57. I believe so much in myself.

58. I am no home to failure.

59. I am the Queen of my territory, and I am a
Queen with pride.

60. I win.

61. I am better than I was yesterday.

62. I have all that I need to have a perfect day.

63. Today is a blessing.

64. Today is full of productivity.

65. I am happy to be alive.

66. I'll smile big smiles today.

67. I am open to learning new things.

68. I am the most wonderful person there is.

69. I know my worth.

70. I do not allow myself to be trampled upon.

71. I am in control.

72. Nothing can stop me from smashing today's
goals.

73. I smash my goals with ease.

74. I am ready for today's success.

75. Today is a wonderful day.

76. I am positive about today.

77. I'll grow in new dimensions today.

78. I am elegance in human form.

79. I am full of peace.

80. Nothing can stop me.

81. I cheer myself into excellence.

82. I am full of intelligence and brilliant ideas.

83. I am super strong.

84. I am deserving of greatness.

85. I do not live in regrets.

86. I step into this day with new energy and warmth.

87. I do not focus on yesterday's failures.

88. Today is the best day of my life.

89. Today is a great day to try again.

90. I am strengthened enough to face today.

91. I will have a fulfilling day.

92. I live this day with power and strength.

93. I find joy in the small things.

Key Points

Do you feel these affirmations in your bones? Yes, I want you to feel them all. You have all it takes to have a day as beautiful as you desire. Today, step into the goodness of the day with these affirmations. I have curated the key points that you should remember often. Read them below!

- The beauty of your day is dependent on you.
- You have all it takes to have a wonderful day.
- Call your day blessed, and it will manifest that blessing.
- You are full of strength, remember this.
- You excel in great measures when you take all responsibility for yourself and your day.

Now that we are done with this beginning, let us saunter into a chapter that is set out to empower you as much as you desire. Shall we begin?

Chapter One

Affirmations for The Empowerment of
The Black Woman

*The empowerment of black women constitutes
the empowerment of our entire community.
-Kimberle Williams Crenshaw*

When I say black women empowerment is a
necessity for the growth of society, I do not
mean any jokes. It is one truth that we all must
embrace. It is saddening that some parts of our
world are yet to embrace the magic that is
black women empowerment. I'm writing the
first chapter of this book for black women
empowerment and for all the struggles that

black women have had to face in their quest to create a better society.

Once, I met a black woman crying on a bus. She looked so pained and troubled. I tried to get close to her when we both alighted. There was something about her that kept on pulling me to her. She smiled at me and wiped off the tears after I calmed her down. Then she told me her story. She said she was being oppressed at work by her superior colleagues just because she refused to bow to their crazy rules and tough working conditions at a low pay. In her words, 'they made me understand that I was asking for too much. That I wasn't worth all that…' she broke into tears before she could finish up what she was saying. Even with all that pain and anger, the young woman wouldn't bow to a thing that like that. I found it really beautiful. I left her with a hug and some words of encouragement.

I know there are lots of women like the one I encountered on the bus. Women going through stress and getting disrespected while at it. Women shrinking themselves for small people. Women dimming their lights to entertain people with small minds. It it is for these women that I write these black women empowerment affirmations in this chapter. For the women in business and the corporate world, the women in quest of success and the women just starting out in business. This chapter is all yours! Come with me as I take you through affirmations just for you.

Business Affirmation

1. Today, I excel in my work spaces.
2. I attract wonderful contracts with good pay.
3. I am large enough to contain all of the things I seek.
4. I have an active brain that can conjure up the best business ideas.
5. I am an overflowing well of intelligence.
6. I do not falter in my pursuit for business excellence.
7. My black excellence precedes me and no workspace can steal that from me.
8. I welcome good jobs and offers into my life.
9. Toxic workspaces would flee at the sight of me.
10. I am too big to accommodate small minds.
11. My business blooms despite all hurdles and discouragement.

12. I am the queen in my kingdom and nothing on earth can bring me down.

13. I am in control of my businesses.

14. The market conditions would tilt towards helping me fulfil my goals.

15. I am made for so much more.

16. I am a breathing body of excellence.

17. I am worthy of the best working conditions.

18. I wine and dine with the best people in my industry.

19. I seal the best business deals with grace and ease.

20. I'll not be broken by my quest for better opportunities.

21. I don't write business applications in vain.

22. I am ready to take over my industry with my intelligence and business sense.

23. My best is more than enough.

24. I do not labour to be left empty in the end.

25. I invite ease into my workspace

26. There is no room for toxicity in my business.

27. My customers will come back to me because I offer the best kind of value.

28. I grow everyday and I excel in the newest things.

29. I open my business to the best grants and developments.

30. My business works in sync with the emancipation of other black women from bad jobs.

31. I bounce back much greater from falls and setbacks.

32. I don't lose my business to fear.

33. My zeal grows.

34. I am not shallow minded.

35. My business acumen opens great doors for me.

36. My workspace is rid of every oppression.

37. I welcome great team members into my space.

38. I don't struggle to shine.

39. I am so much of an asset to be ignored.

40. No amount of work pressure has the power to end me.

41. I give no power to any boss who desires to make me shrink into myself.

42. I lead in the workspace.

43. Being a woman is no limitation for me.

44. History would write my name in bold prints for the good work I do.

45. I take charge of my business today. I leave nothing to chance.

46. Good jobs will find me with ease.

47. I do excellent work. There is no space for mediocre things in me.

48. I am ready to learn new skills and implement the knowledge into the betterment of my businesses.

49. The losses I record do not define the future of my business.

50. My mistakes are not the only things there are to me. I am so much more.
51. I am uniquely creative.
52. I'll utilize my skills and talents in my journey towards excellence.
53. I have all the courage I need to do what I want.
54. I will take advantage of every opportunity to learn and improve on myself.
55. I am ever willing to do the needed work to achieve my goals.
56. I am deserving of security in my finances.
57. I am never going to live from hand to mouth.
58. I manifest the life of my dreams.
59. I welcome financial abundance into my life.
60. My destiny lies in my own hands.
61. I create my own success.
62. All of my dreams are achievable.

63. I have value to offer.

64. I market my skills and not self-pity.

65. My hard work pays off in a hundred folds.

66. I have all it takes to reach the heights I desire.

Key Points

There are essential points that you must note in this session. I understand that you may not be able to memorize all of these affirmations in a single read. This is why I'm making the major affirmations you need to remind yourself of everyday into beautiful and lucid key points that your mind can recall with ease. Whenever your workplace begins to cause you pain or when the empowerment of self becomes difficult, say this to yourself with all the boldness in the world and forge ahead like the Queen that you are.

- You have all it takes to be fully
  empowered.
- You too can thrive amidst all the
  hurdles, negativity and stress.
- You have the power to change your life
  for the best.
- The emancipation of the black woman is
  true freedom.
- You are powerful enough to create the
  life of your dreams.
- Your creativity flows in abundance.

Do you feel like an underachiever sometimes? It's not a foreign feeling to me at all. I'd look around me and find everyone excelling at something, but I'm not. The thing is this; other people would see the things I do and call them success. But they don't even impress me in any way. That is the thing with black women. They are high fliers and lovers of success. They love to make huge impacts in their respective fields. Be it business or entrepreneurship. The corporate space is not left out too. Black women go all out for excellence or nothing. You know the popular phrase saying 'go big or go home?' Black women heard it, and they listened. And they took it literally.

But if we keep on overlooking how far we have come and focusing only on the things we want at the moment, it could ruin us in many ways. Don't you think so? For instance, you want a job at a big firm so much that you put all of your energy into getting the job. Your hard work pays off and you get this job. Two years later, you see a much bigger firm that you are interested in. You try to get into the firm on your first attempt, but you don't. Instead of getting depressed over the rejection, why not try a different approach?

Commend yourself for trying, then you look out for the mistakes you made and things you didn't do well. Then you restrategize and try again. Doing this would get you the job faster because you won't make the same mistakes ever again. This is way better than gloating. This, my dear, is the right approach to success. Your determination, hard work and faith in yourself is all that matters. And never forget how far you have come.

There is no force equal to a woman determined to rise- W.E.B Dubois.

Remember this quote often and let it reaffirm your belief in yourself. You are a force. A very great one. When you set out to achieve a thing, there's nothing that can stop you unless you give it the permission to do so. Yes, you are that powerful. We will affirm success into the whole of our beings in this section. So, let's dive into some success affirmations in style.

Success Affirmations

1. Success knows me by my name.
2. My failure is not the end of the road for me.
3. I rise into my greatness like the morning sun.
4. I succeed in every aspect of my life.
5. I am a force that can never bend to failure.

6. I do not quit, I try again, and I win.
7. I have all it takes to be successful in this life.
8. I disengage myself and all that is mine from failure.
9. I succeed in my finances.
10. I succeed in my relationships.
11. I open myself to relationships that would lead me to my success.
12. Success is my destiny.
13. I am not fated to be a failure.
14. I am a winner, and I'll do what winners do. Win.
15. I succeed even in places where people struggle.
16. I step into my greatness with so much elegance.
17. I am smart.
18. I dictate all that goes on in my life.
19. I make good decisions.
20. I stand up to my fears.

21. I stand up to everything working against my success.

22. I shut out every self-sabotaging thought from my mind.

23. I cleanse my heart of negative thoughts.

24. I have the strength I need to get my heart desires.

25. I am invincible.

26. Nothing on earth has the power to break me.

27. I utilize my potential to the fullest.

28. I give my all to good causes

29. I step out of the norm.

30. I am not made for small things.

31. I am large enough to accommodate big things.

32. I work hard at my goals and aspirations.

33. I will not be found sleeping when I should be working.

34. I am my own competition.

35. I draw strength from all the times that I have had to try again.

36. My success is not measured by that of others.

37. No one has the power to bring me down.

38. I give myself the permission to stretch my creativity as much as I desire.

39. I am worthy of greatness.

40. I am worthy of all the good things I worked for.

41. Mediocrity has no place in my life.

42. I am the standard.

43. I am becoming the successful black woman I have always dreamed of.

44. I embrace my strengths and I work on my weaknesses.

45. I accept my weaknesses. They don't define me.

46. I am the most intelligent woman in the room.

47. My determination pays off in grand styles.

48. My big dreams are coming to fruition.

49. My dreams are valid and that is what matters.

50. I flourish on every side.

51. I bloom on the roughest grounds.

52. I am not consumed by fear.

53. I will climb all the high places I want to be in with no fear.

54. Success clings to me.

55. My success is not a one time thing. It is my lifestyle.

56. I take advantage of opportunities.

57. I breathe excellence.

58. I am growing on every side.

59. I accommodate no sub-standard things.

60. I am originality in all its forms.

61. I have an active brain.

62. I create the opportunities.

63. My success doesn't rest on anyone but me.

64. No one can pull me down.

65. Everything works in my favor.

66. I am sought after because of my
    greatness.
67. I am the best in my field.
68. I excel much more than I dreamt of.
69. I am living my biggest dream.
70. No one can belittle me.
71. I have a functional head on my
    shoulders. I am not shallow nor empty.

Key Points

I bet you love these success affirmations. They are all yours, make sure to use them to the fullest. When obstacles threaten to hinder your success, affirm these and watch everything play out in your favor. Below are the key points for this section.

- You possess all that you need to become successful.
- You excel the most when you embrace your strengths and weaknesses

- You have the ability to stretch yourself as much as you want.
- Your brain is a reservoir of success, you only have to use it optimally.
- Success knows you by your name.

Affirmations For The Black Woman Who Is Just Starting Out In Business

A big business starts small.
—Richard Branson

A lot of black women shy away from starting their own businesses because of fear. You know, fear is so powerful that it can make the best women doubt their own intelligence. But, fear won't overpower you unless you give it the permission to do so. I understand that you are afraid to start because you are afraid it would flop. I understand that there is a lot of competition in the business space. I understand that you want to have a big structure first. I understand that you want nothing short of perfection.

But, you must understand that none of these can even happen if you don't begin at all. Business is a lot of risk, but the risk is worth taking, trust me. You might decide to shut away your business dreams by working for someone else. But this won't lead to the actualization of your own dream, would it? It's either you build your own dream or you build someone else's. That's how it works. I'm pretty sure it is your own dream that you desire to build and not someone else's.

Your fears are valid, but you can overcome them by going into business prepared. How can this preparation be done? Take your time and study about business, take courses, learn from the experts and study the market. Mind you, doing all these doesn't guarantee that you'd make no losses. Rather, it reduces the occurrence of the losses and helps you manage them better when they happen.

Business is a game of profits and losses. Let this stick to your mind.

In this section, I'll take you through powerful affirmations that'll strengthen you as you begin your start up. Yes, you can excel well in business too. Or, don't you remember that anything black is synonymous with excellence? Now, come with me as I affirm the most positive affirmations for your new business!

1. My business is full of ease.
2. I succeed with grace.
3. Everyday, I get closer to my biggest dream.
4. My small business is preparing me for my big business.
5. I start small and end big.
6. My business is the best there is.
7. I attract supportive people.
8. I'll record more and more profits.
9. I believe in my vision.

10. I can achieve anything I put my mind to.

11. My business will know no hurdles.

12. I celebrate my growth and how far I have come.

13. I did not come this far to end here.

14. I have the ability to transform obstacles into opportunities.

15. There are no limitations to how far I can go.

16. My plans come to pass with ease.

17. I love and enjoy my business.

18. I am on the path that leads to fulfillment.

19. I am on the path that leads to the actualization of purpose.

20. Stumbling stones are stepping stones to me.

21. I am not consumed by the challenges that new businesses face.

22. I am found in the places that I need to be.

23. My business opens great doors for me.

24. I am at the place I am supposed to be.

25. Negativity has no place in me.
26. All the work I put in is coming back to me with great results.
27. I excel a lot more than my former self.
28. I reach my zenith with great ease.
29. I leverage on my strengths and work on my weak points.
30. I build my own dreams and not someone else's.
31. I have enough strength and zeal to do what it takes for the betterment of my business.
32. I attract the perfect customers.
33. I am confident in my abilities to excel.
34. I create the best name for myself in my business.
35. I dissociate myself and my business from all negative energies.
36. I do not struggle to be seen. I am as visible as the sun.
37. I am grateful for how far I have come and for the places I am reaching.

38. I manifest my financial goals.

39. I take advantage of every opportunity.

40. I am strengthened by all the times I have had to try again.

41. I derive joy and peace from my business.

42. My clients love what I do.

43. I make great investments.

44. I am not broken by market fluctuations.

45. Impossibility is non-existent in my space.

46. I manage my business on my own terms.

47. I make the best decisions for my business.

48. I attract hardworking people.

49. I am blessed with enough resources.

50. I am driven by passion.

51. I am unyielding to weakness and hopelessness.

52. I attract loyal and responsible customers.

53. I retain customers with ease.

54. I am a passionate and reliable business person.

55. I meet my business targets before the deadlines.

56. I accomplish difficult tasks with smiles on my face.

57. I am enthusiastic about achieving my goals.

58. I break new records every day.

59. Money flows into my business from every corner.

60. I open my business to abundance and huge profits.

61. I am financially secure.

62. All my dreams are coming true.

63. I don't try too hard before I win.

64. Excellence is by lifestyle.

65. I have all the emotional intelligence I need to interact well with my clients.

66. I have all I need to expand my business as much as I want to.

67. My vision is my drive.

68. My name is mentioned when the greats are mentioned.

69. No one does it better than me.

70. My strategies are more than efficient to help me in the actualization of my dreams.

Key Points

This section is all about the black woman starting out in business. I know these affirmations will strengthen you as much as you let it. Below are the key points for this session.

- You'll excel more in business if you prepare before going into It.
- Businesses are risks worth taking.
- You have all it takes to be successful in business.

- It is okay to be afraid of venturing into business.
- Small businesses grow to become big businesses.
- You are the captain of your business.
- There are no limitations to how far you can go.

Now that we are done with the first chapter of this book, hold my hand and let us proceed to the second together. This time, it's not about empowerment, not business. It's about the core of our very existence, self-love. Let's dig in!

Chapter Two

I am The Absolute Love of My Own Life; Self-Love And The Black Woman

To fall in love with yourself is the first secret to happiness.
—Robert Morley

How you love yourself is how you teach others to love you.
—Rupi Kaur.

When I talk about self-love, I remember people who think making fancy posts on social media with the caption 'self-love' is all there is to actually loving one's self. No darling, it is way deeper than that. Loving yourself is beyond making posts on it on social media or just muttering you love yourself.

So, what does self-love really entail? Self-love is all about taking care of yourself in all areas. Taking care of your physical body, your mental health and your emotional health. Self-love makes you realize that you come first in your own life. Yes, not even your partner nor your career nor love should come first. That spot is reserved for you and you alone. It is self-love that nudges you to step out of places that shrink you and depreciate you. It is the amount of love that you have for yourself that would show people how to treat you. You don't have to sacrifice your well being for anyone just because you want to make the person comfortable or happy. I remind you again, you come first in your life.

Also, self-love is one of the greatest recipes for true happiness. Robert Morley reaffirms this. He says to fall in love with yourself is the first secret to happiness. Are you unhappy? Could it be that you are yet to fall truly in love with yourself? Yes, it is actually possible not to love one's self. When you neglect your well being and go after things that diminish you, it is a sign that you don't love yourself. And, self-love goes hand in hand with happiness. So, you must first love yourself. It is the first and most important step you need to take in your pursuit of happiness.

One more thing. Self-love doesn't rob you of empathy. You can love yourself and still love other people too. You only have to show yourself a greater amount of love. You know, you can't really love other people well if you don't know how to love yourself. Crazy, right? But it is the one truth. It takes a great amount of self-love to be able to love others. And for this reason, you must love you first. This chapter will be all about self-love and care because I care deeply about your well being. I'll hold you gently in this chapter and guide you as you fall in love with yourself all over again. Let's go!

I Come First In My Own Life.

1. I love myself endlessly.
2. I am the most important person in my life and I treat myself as such.
3. I do not shrink myself to make people feel good.
4. I am not consumed by the negative energies of other people.
5. My well being is my priority.
6. I love myself with all that is in me and all that I am.
7. I am not trampled upon.

8. I am deserving of my own affection and
    care.

9. I fall endlessly in love with myself.

10. I love myself wholly so I can love others.

11. I choose myself.

12. I allow no one to make me feel guilty for
    choosing myself.

13. I matter greatly.

14. I am the number one in my own life.

15. I am exceedingly great and important.

16. I care for myself with grace and ease.

17. I glow with love.

18. I invest in myself because I am my
    greatest asset.

19. I am so full of love and warmth.

20. I love myself fully and I hold back
    nothing.

21. I am generous with self-care.

22. I take breaks when necessary.

23. I take a rest when I get tired. I will not
    quit.

24. I am the best cheerleader I could ever have.

25. I embrace myself with elegance.

26. I am more than enough.

27. I am the truest love of my life.

28. I grow into the best version of myself.

29. I love myself more everyday.

30. I am the most gorgeous person on earth.

31. I am beautifully unique.

32. I am surrounded by pure love.

33. Loving myself is easy for me.

34. I am worthy of love.

35. I love myself with no reservations.

36. I do not struggle to accept myself.

37. I am the best thing that can happen to me.

38. I am a body of beauty and perfection.

39. I am deserving of all the care that I get.

40. I am my topmost priority.

41. I am the best there is.

42. I am the brightest star there is.

43. I do not soil myself with hate and toxicity.
44. I love myself enough to walk out of negative spaces.
45. I love myself enough to walk away from people who do not love me.
46. I am the greatest validation I could ever seek.
47. I am the perfection I crave.
48. I care for my mental health with ease.
49. I love myself no matter what happens.
50. I am so full of love to accommodate any strand of hate.
51. My love for myself flows like a river.

Key Points

This section is written to remind you that you come first in your own life. Yes, you are the loveliest love of your own life. Never let anyone tell you otherwise. I have made this section into brief and concise points that you should recall and dwell in as often as you can.

- You come first in your own life.
- People can only love you as much as you love yourself.
- You are deserving of love and affection.
- You become happier when you learn to love yourself with no reservations.
- You are the greatest validation you could ever seek.
- You should never shrink yourself to make people happy at your own expense.
- You are worth it. You are more than enough.

Loving Myself Again After A Terrible Experience.

In order to love who you are, you cannot hate the experiences that shaped you.
—Andrea Dykstra.

Have you ever hated yourself, dear black woman? Do you hate yourself? Asking these questions feels weird, right? When people are asked if they hate themselves, the most popular reaction is a cursory look and some wonderment. I mean, why would you hate yourself? Does this imply that there are people who do not hate themselves?

Just as there are people who love themselves with all of their beings, there are also people who hate themselves deeply. I know you're getting more interested here. People hate themselves for different reasons. For some, self-hate could be sponsored by illnesses like depression and the likes. For some, the hate stems from a feeling of worthlessness. You know, feeling like you aren't worth a thing. Feeling at the bottom of the world. Feeling like you belong to the decrepit. And for some, the hate stems from bad experiences and not so good choices.

This section is going to be focused only on this last category of people. People who hate themselves for the choices and mistakes they made. Mistakes and regrets make a fine and strong pair because the latter comes after the former. But, you must understand that both of them are parts of our existence. We can't eliminate them totally, but we surely can avoid them and we also have the power not to let them decide our lives for us. Yes, I'm powerful like that. You too are powerful. Much more than you know.

Like Andrea Dykstra made us know in the beginning of this section, you cannot love yourself if you go about detesting the experiences that shaped you. You cannot experience the full impact of love for self if you keep on gloating about your mistakes. You have to embrace them as a part of your life. Then you forge ahead and love yourself. This, my dear, is how it all works. So, let's go on another self-love and acceptance trip. Shall we?

Affirmations On Loving Myself Again After All of My Mistakes and Bad Choices

1. My mistakes and terrible choices do not define my whole life.
2. I see my mistakes as stepping stones that led me to the actualization of my truest self.
3. I love myself despite my errors and flaws.
4. I love and accept myself wholly.
5. I learn from my mistakes.
6. I accept all of the things that shaped me.
7. I am the best version of myself.
8. I cherish myself greatly.
9. I do not repeat my mistakes.
10. I am grateful for the learning experience my bad choices offered me.
11. I am not consumed by my mistakes.
12. My heart is healed of all the pains my mistakes caused me.

13. I refuse to wallow in pain and self-pity.

14. I am exceedingly kind to myself.

15. I am so full of love.

16. My life is beautiful.

17. I find joy in living.

18. My heart overflows with peace.

19. I am very proud of who I am becoming.

20. I have the unique ability to create the love I need and dwell in it.

21. I have made peace with my past self.

22. I do not wallow in the past for I do not belong there anymore.

23. I do not judge myself for the mistakes I have made.

24. I embrace joy in abundance.

25. I am unapologetically myself and that is enough.

26. I choose myself everyday.

27. I have inner peace and nothing can take it away from me.

28. I do not give my past the power to steal my joy.

29. There is so much love inside me.

30. I am the best of my kind.

31. I am powerful.

32. I meet my expectations with ease.

33. My mistakes do not reduce my worth.

34. I am not ashamed to seek help.

35. I pay great attention to my body and its needs

36. I trust in all of my abilities.

37. I do not go back to the things that broke me.

38. I love the woman I see in the mirror everyday.

39. I bear so much in me and I will shine brilliantly for all the world to see.

40. I throw away all the negative baggage that delays my journey.

41. I am full of strength.

42. I love myself and all that I am fiercely.

43. I protect myself from all forms of toxicity.

44. My soul is home to a lot of beauty.

45. I bloom with so much grace.

46. I thrive everywhere.

47. I write my story with joy.

48. I am gentle and loving to myself.

49. I sing my best songs and live my best days.

50. I attract kindness and love.

We have come to the end of this chapter. I hope you enjoyed our journey through it. Before we begin another trip of affirmations in the next chapter, I'll leave you with key points for this section. Dig in!

Key Points

- Your mistakes and bad choices do not define you.
- You can rise again from the most terrible events.

- Happiness begins the moment you embrace all of the events that shaped you into your present self.
- You are more than enough.
- Seeking help is no weakness.
- Tell your story with pride. Own it.

Chapter Three

Anxiety And Its Throes

Worrying doesn't empty tomorrow of its sorrow, it empties today of its strength.
—Corrie Ten Boom.

Everyone of us has experienced anxiety in our lives one way or the other. You know, it is our nature to panic, worry and get troubled over things that bother us. We love solutions and not problems. Before I go on and on about anxiety and its throes, it'll be beautiful if I explain what anxiety means in very lucid terms, right? I'll do just that.

Anxiety is a disorder that's characterized by excessive worrying, panic attacks, fright, abnormal sweating and lots of other factors.

Anxiety arises when we try to meet up with expectations, do stuff right, meet deadlines. All these and every other thing that has the tendency to bother you and steal your peace can lead to anxiety. A lot of black women often wonder if anxiety can set in independently. This is almost impossible because anxiety must have a trigger. Your own thoughts and imaginations can trigger anxiety in you. Other people can make you anxious too.

When I was younger, I used to have this crush who made me feel butterflies. I never confessed to the crush because I feared getting rejected so much. I'd tell my friends all about what I felt but I never told the crush. I felt a lot of anxiety. Maybe I'd have not felt all that anxiety if I ever confessed to the crush. Who knows? My friends would always egg me on to confess to the crush. I'd get sweaty palms and itchy armpits because of anxiety. What am I driving that? I'm letting you know that emotions also have the ability to trigger anxiety. In fact, emotions are one of the most powerful things ever. Tell me, have you ever broken a resolve because your emotions came into play? See? Emotions are very powerful, and they can overwhelm you easily if you do not learn how to tame them. Anxiety can mess up your mental health if you give it the chance to do it.

You can overcome anxiety by dealing with that one thing that triggers it. If you try to stop the anxiety without first dealing with the triggers, you might as well be fighting a losing battle. So, gorgeous soul, you have to first deal with the causes of your anxiety. Funny thing is some of these triggers are not things that can be easily eliminated. Say work deadlines for example, they would always be there. In cases like that, try to remind yourself of the power and mastery that you possess. Why worry about a deadline that you'd meet in the end? No reason at all! Worrying only robs you of strength and joy, try your possible best not to indulge it every time.

The good news is that you don't have to bear the burdens of anxiety all alone. I'll help you overcome it and become the relaxed and graceful Queen that you are through affirmations written just for you. Hold my hand and let's begin!

Affirmations for Strength Against Anxiety.

1. I am much stronger and powerful than my anxiety.
2. I meet my deadlines with ease and grace.
3. I do not stutter while presenting my incredible ideas.
4. Everything works in my favor.
5. Nothing is out to hunt me down.
6. I am safe, nobody is after my life.

7. My past experiences have no power over my success.

8. I am relaxed.

9. I have the power to restore calmness to my life.

10. I am calm and hopeful.

11. I refuse to panic.

12. There is no fear in my veins but courage and strength.

13. I can overcome anything in the world.

14. I am set out for victory.

15. I create paths in blocked places.

16. I have survived a lot of bad days. I'll survive this one too.

17. Stress has no power nor control over my life.

18. I do not palpitate when all I need to do is think.

19. I breathe with ease.

20. There is so much happiness in my life.

21. I can handle this one too.

22. Success knows my name and it calls me in a loud voice.

23. I am in control of my life.

24. I am in control of the situation.

25. I am beautiful and I am deeply loved.

26. I distance myself from panic and fear.

27. I am patient enough to handle the most difficult situations.

28. I breathe out all the fear holding me back.

29. I take up difficult tasks without breaking a sweat.

30. I can sail above anxiety.

31. I eliminate all that triggers my anxiety with elegant ease.

32. I have so much talent and I put it into use by doing good work.

33. I am a badass.

34. I'm indefatigable. Nothing can break me.

35. I am too defiant to be broken by anxiety.

36. I pay no heed to the lies that anxiety tells me.

37. I shut out all the negative voices in my head.

38. I guard my sanity with all my might.

39. I control my breaths as much as I want to.

40. I do good work without getting broken.

41. I have no doubts about the value I offer.

42. I get great jobs because I am amazing at what I do.

43. I talk about my brand with all the courage in the world.

44. The faith I have in myself is enough.

45. Negative thoughts do not belong with me.

46. I am larger than my anxiety.

47. I do not give in to irrational fear.

48. I give my best to my job and I do not flop at it.

49. My best is enough.

50. I grow my brand with zeal and joy.

Key Points

My dear, I believe this section has strengthened you against anxiety and its troubles. You can overcome anxiety when you acknowledge the power you possess. With this power, kill anxiety and live your life with ease. I have curated a few salient points that you should recall often. Find them below!

- You are bigger than your anxiety.
- You have all it takes to end your anxiety.
- Anxiety does nothing positive for you. Rather, it robs you of your peace and hinders your productivity.
- Anxiety is inevitable sometimes, but you have the power to shut it out.
- The faith you have in yourself is more than enough.
- Everyone isn't set out to cause your downfall like anxiety made you believe.

Anxiety Management Affirmations For The Overwhelmed Black Woman

Sometimes, everything becomes overwhelming. Most people think anxiety comes in only when things are going wrong. No, this is not true at all. You can also become anxious when things are going just fine for you.

Sometimes, I get overwhelmed with all the good days and wonder why I was having a lot of good days. Sounds crazy, right? But this is actually a thing. Good days can be as overwhelming as bad days. Also, anxiety can also set in when you have a standard to maintain. For example, you are the best student in your school. Getting the best result is your standard, your lifestyle. Even without trying so hard, you'd subconsciously desire to maintain that standard or supersede it even. Performing below your standard could lead to a lot of anxiety for you.

When anxiety begins to steal the shine in your life, don't make the mistake of waiting for it to go away. Deal with it the very moment it steps in. Deal with the disturbing thought and deal with the panic before it grows into something you cannot handle easily. Also, remind yourself that you are the boss. Bosses take charge, you take charge. Speak to that anxiety and have it bow to your command. Affirmations can help you manage your anxiety as much as you want. So, come with me let us walk with all elegance through these anxiety management affirmations.

1. I manage my anxiety with ease.
2. I take charge of my responsibilities well.
3. I am deserving of all the good things that happen to me.
4. I do not run away from taking big steps.
5. I make good decisions.
6. I am not overwhelmed by worries.
7. I do not attract stress and hard labour.
8. I am excellent at managing my anxiety.
9. I don't give up when it gets tough.
10. I have enough time to chase my priorities.
11. I give all my attention to the things that matter.
12. I am in control of all my emotions.
13. I starve myself of my distractions.

14. I dissociate myself from everything that stops me from doing my duties well.

15. I manage my time effectively to accommodate all that I need to do.

16. I step into my powers with ease.

17. I do not know how to give up.

18. My anxiety can never steal my shine.

19. I stand tall despite my anxiety.

20. I bounce back bigger and better.

21. I am deserving of every good thing I get.

22. I can fix this one too.

23. I am great at handling things.

24. I do not bow to pressure.

25. I go through this difficult phase and come out unscathed.

Key Points

- You have all it takes to control your anxiety.
- Anxiety doesn't last forever, neither does pressure. You'll get through them.
- You are deserving of good things, do not let them overwhelm you.
- You are great at dealing with your responsibilities.

Affirmations For Black Women Battling Anxiety

Every day, thousands of black women battle with anxiety in various forms. In their homes, workplaces, personal lives and a myriad of other places. Dealing with any form of mental trouble could be so overwhelming sometimes. Also, people do not really seem to understand mental illnesses and how they affect people. This is why you'll always find people who ridicule people with mental illnesses. But, this shouldn't discourage you from getting help when you should.

A lot of studies have shown that getting help early enough for mental illnesses increases your chances of recovering faster and better. The moment you realize that something is wrong, do not shield it. Get help. It is actually a thing of great courage to get help for mental illnesses. I am not unaware of that at all.

Also, don't feel bad for anything at all. It happens to the best of us too. Do not let anyone shame you into keeping mum about your situation. It is very detrimental. Not to you alone, but also to your family and loved ones. Believe me when I say you can pull through your anxiety.

Do not be afraid. You won't deal with it all alone. I am here for you like I have always been. I'll hold you tightly as you walk on the beautiful and rough road that leads to healing. Let us begin.

1. I have all it takes to pull through my anxiety.
2. Getting the help I need is not synonymous to weakness.
3. I am worth it. I have always been.
4. Anxiety won't end me. I will end it.
5. I have all the courage I need to receive help.

6. Anxiety is not the end of my life.

7. I am a fighter, I'll fight this and win.

8. I am not ashamed to get help.

9. I fill my life with peace.

10. I refuse to be bothered by little things.

11. I dissociate myself from negativity.

12. I identify the root causes of my anxiety with ease.

13. I give no one the power and permission to shame me with my condition.

14. I do not surrender to my weaknesses.

15. I'll let no one trigger me.

16. I move away from my triggers with ease.

17. I have the ability to concentrate only on the things that matter.

18. I am amazing and loved.

19. My eyes are fixated on the beauty of my existence.

20. I do not struggle to get help.

21. I have the strength and courage to get therapy.

22. I walk boldly towards healing.

We have come to the end of this chapter. Did you have fun going through these anxiety affirmations? I bet you did. In the next chapter, we'll explore the beauty of sleep and wonderful sleep affirmations curated just for you. Turn the page and read on. I've got so much in store for you!

Chapter Four

The Value of Sleep To The Black Woman.

Sleep is like the golden chain that binds our health and body together.
—Thomas Dekker

I've had people ask for my skincare routine a lot of times. I have this gorgeous and silky skin that makes people stare at me more than once. When I hear people say there is no such thing as perfect skin, I resist the urge to walk up to them, pull them close and show them my skin. Yes, my skin is a thing of beauty. And in the words of John Keats, a thing of beauty is a joy forever. I know you too are interested in finding out the magic to the perfection in my skin. It is not on the high side, so you too can try it out. My ultimate skin care routine is good sleep. Sleeping as I should. Sleeping fully. No, I'm not making this up. There is something that adequate sleep does to your skin that not even the most expensive products can. Good sleep gives you a natural glow. That irresistible glow that comes with being a black woman.

But then, is a glowing skin all there is to good sleep? Of course not. There is a lot more to it. Various studies have shown that people are more productive when they get adequate sleep. I've tried this on myself, and I've gotten a lot of proof. I am the most productive when I get as much sleep as my body needs. This may sound quite unbelievable to you, but it is one of those truths that you should remember very often. You know, we deceive ourselves sometimes and overwork ourselves because we feel taking needed sleep would slow us down. We neglect the fact that getting sleep would help us a lot with our productivity and general output. Our bodies are made to require sleep. It is a necessity. Some people would try to make us feel bad for sleeping as though sleeping is a sin and not a healthy thing to do. Don't let anyone make you feel bad for sleeping. If anyone tries to, you might as well educate the person on the importance of sleep. Not only does it make you glow, it is also better for your health. As you make plans for your parties and meetings and dates, also make plans for sleep. Your body and health would be forever grateful to you. Do you see all the good work adequate sleep does for your body?

Some people wonder if sleep affirmations actually work considering that we are 'inactive' while asleep. You know, we're not doing any form of work while sleeping. This is a very wrong notion to follow. The main purpose of sleep is rest and rejuvenation. So, yes. The affirmations would work just fine even if you sleep. Affirmations are not as complex as we make them out to be sometimes. So, make your affirmations at any time you want. But somehow, people tend to make sleep affirmations just before they go to bed. I do it too. Saying my sleep affirmations just before bed always fills me with this surge of energy that makes me feel much more power than I am.

One other thing that makes me say my sleep affirmations is this: it helps me relax and empty my mind of the thoughts of the things that happened during the day. I'd climb into my bed and say my affirmations with power before I finally sleep. If you're a person that thinks so much before sleeping, saying your affirmations just before bedtime would do you a lot of good. Don't you think so, too?

I write this section for the sole purpose of opening your eyes and mind to see and understand the importance of sleep. I understand that you might have contrary views buried deeply in your subconscious. But, you and I will eliminate all of them armed with the power that affirmations carry. So, hold my hand one more time as we go on another affirmation journey. Let us explore sleep and all its beauty.

Sleep Affirmations For The Black Woman

1. I'll not let anything rob me of my sleep.
2. I'll sleep as much as I need to.
3. I do not battle with insomnia.
4. I fall asleep with ease.
5. The evidence of my good sleep shows beautifully on my skin.
6. Sleep comes easy to me.
7. I am not awakened by nightmares.
8. I dream beautiful dreams when I sleep.
9. I enjoy sleeping.
10. I make great plans for my sleep.
11. I am not too overwhelmed to lose sleep.

12. I sleep peacefully.

13. I am refreshed when I sleep.

14. I glow differently when I sleep.

15. I suffer no sleep disorder.

16. I give my body the pleasure of sleep.

17. I do not neglect my health by not sleeping when I should.

18. My dreams are filled with hope and positivity.

19. I am deserving of rest.

20. I. choose to sleep and rest. I will try again tomorrow.

21. I am thankful for a healthy body that sleeps with ease.

22. I am safe in my sleep.

23. My sleep strengthens me and fills me with new energy.

24. I wake up to a good body.

25. I wake up joyfully as my most authentic self.

26. I am grateful for all the things I achieved today. My sleep will fill me with more

energy that will help me do better tomorrow.

27. My eyes close in joy.

28. My wellness is top priority to me; I do not neglect my sleep for any reason.

29. Nightmares have no place in my sleep.

30. I begin a new day well rested and refreshed.

31. I am more productive when I get good sleep.

32. I am worthy of great rest.

33. I am in control of how I sleep.

34. I develop healthy and beautiful sleep habits.

35. I do not let the internet make me lose sleep.

36. I enjoy the unique relaxation that sleep alone can give.

37. I am not consumed by anxiety that I'd lose my sleep.

38. I wake up rejuvenated and strong.

39. I empty my mind of thoughts that would keep me up all night.

40. I distance myself from bad sleeping habits.

41. I wake up with a glow, not eye bags.

42. I refuse to see the time I spend sleeping as wasted time.

43. I step into great strength when I sleep.

44. I dream beautiful dreams in my sleep and they come to pass.

45. I do not give anyone the permission to make me feel bad for resting.

46. I fall asleep with a lot of ease.

47. I am healthy and strong.

48. I embrace the beauty and serenity of sleep with my arms wide open.

Key Points

I have singled out the core points that you should remember always in this chapter. Find them below!

- The time you spend sleeping is not wasted time.
- You are worthy of pleasant night rests and the most beautiful of dreams.
- You glow up when you embrace the peace and strength that sleep gives.
- Good sleep enhances your productivity much more than you can ever imagine.
- Good sleep is one of the best skincare products ever. You don't find it in stores.
- Sleep makes you healthy. Embrace it with love.

Good Sleep Is Adequate Self-Care

For many black women, self-care is all about expensive lotions and skincare routines, long hours in the spa and food. Inasmuch as these are essential parts of caring for one's self, they are not all there is to self care. It is much more beyond that.

To care for yourself is to take care of yourself from the inside out. I used to have a very limited view of self-care in the past. The usual skin care, good hair and good food are the kind that a lot of people know. I'd finish going through my routines and still feel drained. I knew that wasn't close to normalcy at all. In fact, it was miles and miles away from it.

I knew I had to do something about it. I needed to experience the relaxation and warmth of true self-care. I wanted to feel something different. Something that was beyond good skin and a beautiful face. It was at that point that I began to take care of myself the most. It wasn't easy one bit because I was used to a certain lifestyle. I had to unlearn, relearn and adapt to new situations. That, my dear, was the beginning of my journey to true and adequate self-care.

In the course of my self-care journey, I discovered a lot of things. One of the best things I discovered was the power of sleep and the role sleep plays in self-care. This is what I want to share with you in this section. You should know that your self-care processes are incomplete without sleep. Why is this so? I'll explain to you in a very lucid way.

Sleep plays a great role in self-care because it is the core of true relaxation. Most of us indulge in self-care processes like massage, manicure and pedicure, exfoliation and others because we see them as avenues through which we can peel stress off our skins. The main purpose of self-care is relaxation and stress relief. When self-care fails to do these well, it would suffice to say that it didn't achieve its purpose. This is why you should embrace sleep. It is one of the most important self-care processes that a lot of us ignore.

It would interest you to know that getting good sleep would make the other self-care processes work better. The body thrives with relaxation and not tension. This is why sleeping well can help you fight eye bags and wrinkles more efficiently than lotions. Doesn't this amaze you? It would take a while for you to adapt to sleeping well if you're used to getting very short sleeps. But, this is one adaptation that you'll be grateful for for a very long time because the goodness it brings lasts for a very long time. This goodness expresses itself through your skin. It glows up your skin. You want to rock gorgeous skin when you're old, don't you? I know you want to. And that is why I urge you to embrace adequate sleep today and make it an essential part of your self-care.

I have curated relaxing self-care affirmations for you in this section. They'll help you rise into the knowledge of true self-care and the great beauty of sleep. Hold my hand tightly, let's go through these affirmations together. It will be worth all the while.

Adequate Sleep And Self-Care Affirmations

1. I take care of myself from the inside out.
2. I embrace good sleep with all that there is in me.
3. Sleep is the core of my self-care processes.
4. I glow up with ease because I have embraced true self-care.

5. True relaxation finds me with grace and ease because I have embraced the power of sleep.
6. Sleep finds me ready every day.
7. I have made sleep the core of my self-care.
8. I do not neglect my self-care for any reason.
9. I invest in my beauty through sleep.
10. Good sleep is one of the most beautiful things that has happened to me.
11. I sleep when I need to.
12. I am grateful for the rejuvenation that sleep gives me.
13. I throw away all the unhealthy self-care processes that I used to embrace.
14. I care for myself with so much love.
15. I do not take my self-care lightly. I am aware of its importance.
16. I do not find it difficult to relax when I want to.
17. I choose to care for myself wholly today.

18. I adapt to healthy changes with ease.

19. My self-care is worth it.

20. I catwalk into the elegance that self-care heralds.

Key Points

I have compiled the most salient points in this section for your ease and reading pleasure. Find them below.

- Good sleep is the core of self-care.
- Good sleep is one of the loveliest skincare products ever.
- Sleeping well makes you glow.
- Sleep rejuvenates a person.

I Deserve All The Sleep that I Can Get

I have met lots of women who feel undeserving of sleep. Yes, this is actually a thing. The question now is, why would anyone feel undeserving of sleep? This could stem from various reasons. The first that I'd tell you about is trauma.

Say a woman's house got burnt while she was asleep, or her child got into great trouble while she slept. Mind you, these are just instances that I am using to drive my point home. Any woman that has experienced any of these would spend a long time healing from the trauma. She'd always find a reason to blame herself for 'letting' it happen. You'll hear her say things like; it happened because I slept. It's all my fault. I can't forgive myself for this.

The woman might even need some therapy to be able to deal with the trauma. The crazier thing is the fact that trauma never really goes away sometimes. It hides somewhere in you and wait patiently for the perfect time to make you aware of its presence in your life. It has a way of making you feel evil in situations where you meant well and tried your best. Now, how long would you let trauma rule your life? How long will you let that guilt thrive? How long will you ditch sleep? Don't tell me it's forever, please.

To combat this guilt that comes with sleeping, you have to first understand that it is not your fault. Yes, it is not your fault. No one makes grievous mistakes deliberately. No normal human loves to self-destruct. You have to accept that what happened happened. Then, you move on the path that leads to healing. Healing is no easy journey, but I trust that you will do well at it. You are a black woman who is powerful enough to do impossible things. As you walk the healing path, you will gradually begin to understand that you deserve your sleep. In fact, you deserve as much sleep as you can possibly get. And you can get it.

Another category of women who feel less deserving of sleep are people who value their productivity so much. You know, those ones that are more than willing to work their asses off to get what they want. Those ones who desire to leave bold marks in this world. Women who thrive on big ambitions and dreams. It is a wonderful thing to do all you can to fulfil your dreams. But it is not a wonderful thing to throw sleep away while at it. Remember the relationship between sleep and productivity that I talked about in a previous section? Sleep enhances productivity. I know it might sound counter-productive to you now. But, it isn't at all. When you sleep well, your body will function optimally. So, my dear woman, remember to sleep well and take necessary rests as you work on smashing those goals. Also, your tribe can manage affairs when you sleep. I understand how well you want to manage everything by being up most of the time. I know you are greatly needed. But, don't let this overwhelm you or make you quit sleeping. Sleep first, then attend to your affairs later. You need a healthy body to do everything well. Don't you think so, too?

This section is all about powerful affirmations for you who feels undeserving of sleep. Walk this affirmation walk with me as I lead you back into good sleep and rest. It is time to welcome rest into yourself again. Shall we begin?

Affirmations for The Black Woman Who Feels Undeserving Of Sleep

1. I welcome absolute rest and good sleep into my body again.
2. I am deserving of all the sleep I get.
3. I thrive the most when I sleep well.
4. I forgive myself for all the times that sleeping caused me to make mistakes.
5. I forgive myself for my mistakes.
6. Sleep fills me with peace.
7. I refuse to see sleep as a synonym for laziness. I am good and strong.
8. I welcome myself into adequate sleep again.
9. I deserve great rest.
10. My body is refueled by the peace and tranquillity of sleep.
11. I am not consumed by the busyness of my day that I would lose my sleep.
12. I am not a superhuman. I sleep to regain energy.

13. I empty my mind of everything that causes me not to sleep well.

14. I am not overwhelmed. I am in control.

15. I do not sleep to wake up lazy.

16. Sleep increases my productivity.

17. I strip my sleep of nightmares and restlessness.

18. I sleep with ease and elegance.

19. I attract the most gorgeous of dreams when I sleep.

20. I deserve the peace I feel when I sleep.

21. I give no one the permission to make me sleepless.

22. I am no insomniac.

23. Sleep looks very beautiful on me.

24. I bloom in my sleep.

Key Points

I believe these affirmations will welcome you back into true rest and graceful sleep. I have curated key points that you should always remember. Try to recall them as often as you can. You'll be glad that you did. Find the key points below.

- You deserve all the sleep that you get.
- Sleeping is not a counter-productive venture, it increases your productivity much more than you know.
- Forgive yourself wholeheartedly for all the times that sleeping made you make mistakes.
- Care for yourself by sleeping well.
- You are no super human, sleep when you have to.
- Your brain thrives greatly with the tranquillity that sleep gives.

We have come to the end of the sleep affirmations. I hope you had a wonderful ride. Now, we'll begin another journey of affirmations. This time, we'll explore beauty affirmations and what beauty really means. Let's go!

Chapter Five

Beauty Affirmations For The Black Woman.

Beauty begins the moment you decide to be yourself.
—Coco Chanel.

Read the above quote carefully. Now, read it again and let your brain absorb it wholly. When people are asked what the definition of beauty is, they'd most likely mention a certain eye color, skin tone, hair texture and even lip type! Have you noticed that some modeling agencies are big perpetrators of these stereotypes? They make it look as though beauty is limited to a certain tribe. But, I am glad about the black women revolution going on in our world today. Now, no one dares to teach us what beauty is or what it should be. It makes me wonder, why do people think beauty is limited to a certain standard? Why do people try to make others feel small because they do not fit into their definition of beauty? No one, dear black woman, has the right to fix you into a box.

I love gardens. Beautiful gardens. In all my years of exploring various garden types and styles, I have come to know this one thing. The most beautiful gardens are those that contain many flowers. There is so much beauty in variety, you know. I see this world as a garden of some sort too. The world is a garden, you and I are the various flowers that make up the garden. The beauty of the garden is largely dependent on the variety between you and I.

The distinction between us is what makes the garden a thing of endless beauty. Whenever anyone tries to make you feel less of yourself for being uniquely beautiful, let the person know this.

Being treated with disdain is one thing a lot of black women have had to deal with at some stages of their lives. This is especially peculiar to the black women who choose to be themselves audaciously. You know, when you refuse to follow the crowd, the crowd would try to make you follow it by intimidating you into submission. But, we are black women whose ancestors do not know how to surrender. I've seen black women being sent out of corporate places and parties for wearing their hair with pride because afros are not presentable. As funny and sad this may sound, it is the truth. In fact, it is but one of the few things that black women go through.

My dear black woman, I want you to know that you are more than enough. Do not give any soul the permission to make you feel like you are not. You are whole and you are more than enough. Let this stick to every part of your heart.

I write this section for all black women who have been made to undergo the torture of beauty stereotypes. Women who hid their truest beauties to fit into societal stereotypes. For you, I write with vigor and joy and revolution. We'll begin a journey of affirmations again. The time has come again for us to speak power into ourselves and flaunt our daring beauties with all the pride there is in the world. Hold my hand, let us begin our affirmation walk!

I Am Enough.

1. My beauty is too large to fit into small boxes.
2. I am as beautiful as I am. I am the best I can be.
3. I love every part of myself.
4. I am more than enough.
5. I teach the sun what it means to shine.
6. I am beautiful forever.
7. I am effortlessly beautiful.
8. I bear so much positivity inside me that it glows on my skin.
9. My skin gives gorgeous a new and brighter meaning.
10. I do not compare myself to anyone.
11. I exude great beauty and charm.
12. I glow with effortless grace.
13. My soul is beautiful.
14. I am a breathing perfection.
15. I love how I look.
16. I am beautiful on the inside and the outside.

17. No one can make me feel small.

18. I do not embrace the world's stereotypes on beauty.

19. Everything about me is art.

20. I care for my skin with ease.

21. Being beautiful is no struggle for me.

22. I fall in love with the magic that I am everyday.

23. I love the shape of my body.

24. I wear my skin with pride and confidence.

25. My beauty attracts wonderful people.

26. I light up the world with my beauty.

27. I am my most original self.

28. I am audaciously elegant.

29. I create my own style.

30. I do not live on public approval. My approval is all that I need.

31. I have an irresistible charm.

32. My smile has a lot of beauty.

33. I am a perfect combination of rare intelligence and elegance.

34. I am the Queen of my territory.

35. I am grateful for all my features.

36. People are attracted to me.

37. I have the most gorgeous pair of eyes.

38. The texture of my hair is standard.

39. I am hot and I know it.

40. I have a graceful carriage.

41. No one can shrink my amazing self.

42. I make every dress beautiful and perfect.

43. I am the sexiest woman there is.

44. I make everything around me exceedingly beautiful.

Key Points

In the words of John Keats, a thing of beauty is a joy forever. I want you to remember this everyday because you are a thing of beauty. You are enough. Beautiful and enough. Below are the key points I curated specially for you in this section.

- You are the best kind of beautiful.

- You are unique in your own way, don't
  let anyone make you feel otherwise.

- You are too spectacular to fit into any
  stereotypical boxes.

- You teach the sun the art of shining.

- You are enough, and that is all that
  matters.

I Accept Myself

Dr. Steve Maraboli said; *When I accept myself, I am freed from the burden of needing you to accept me.*

This is one of the most beautiful quotes I have ever seen on self-acceptance. A lot of people go on and on about self-acceptance without even knowing what it is. Self-acceptance is more than just telling people to take you as you are or saying you can't change for anyone. To accept yourself is to embrace the whole of you. The perfections, the flaws and everything in between.

It is human nature to seek validation from other humans. It is one of the most burdensome things I have ever known. You know, I used to think that it was possible to be truly loved by everyone. How wrong I was. I realized the impossibility of being a sweetheart to everyone quite early in life, and I am very grateful for it.

If you are among the people who are yet to realize it or people who realized it quite late, don't feel bad at all. Growth is beautiful irrespective of when it happens. Each and everyone of us is made of different pleasing and displeasing characteristics. Some of the features we consider very pleasant could be quite disgusting to other people. This is why it is impossible for you to please everyone. Trying to please everyone is like trying to keep water in a basket. It never works.

It is for this reason that you must accept yourself. Embrace yourself with all of your good and bad. When you accept yourself, you loosen yourself from the sorrow that is embedded in seeking acceptance from other people. Also, you must accept yourself first before other people can accept you. Self-acceptance is not an easy thing at all, but it is a very wonderful thing to do. It'll help you love yourself and appreciate your uniqueness more.

Begin your self-acceptance by making peace with the fact that you are a human who makes mistakes and not some robot that is designed to do everything a certain way. When you make peace with this fact, every other thing becomes easier. Then, you begin to embrace yourself with open arms. Don't be selective in your embrace, please. Do well to embrace the perfection in your waistline, the music in your voice, the small breasts, the shy face, the dreamy eyes. Every single thing. You know, it takes a fine blend of flaw and perfection to flesh out elegance.

When you've accepted all of you, you'll see all the charm and magic that you are. You don't have to worry at all about going on your self-acceptance journey all alone. I'm with you to hold your hands and help you navigate through the rough paths. Through every affirmation that this section will be home to, I hold your hand to show my solidarity and to guide you. Now, let us begin.

Beauty Affirmations For Self-Acceptance

1. I love all of my features.
2. I am the best version of myself.
3. I am uniquely beautiful
4. I love the kind of woman that I am.
5. I am beautiful in every part.
6. I am a flawed perfection.
7. No one's opinion of me matters to me.
8. I love and accept all that there is to me.
9. I forgive myself for all the times I let people's definition of me steal my joy.
10. I send peace, acceptance and courage to my doubts.
11. I do not stay in toxicity to get accepted.
12. Every part of me plays a great role in who I am. So I embrace every part with love and kindness.

13. I quit apologizing for being myself.

14. I am full of confidence.

15. I do not seek for validations in places I cannot find it.

16. The only approval of myself I value and cherish is my own.

17. I nurture my body with care and attention.

18. I absolutely adore my body.

19. I celebrate the wonders of myself everyday.

20. I sing my best songs without apologizing to anyone on how my voice sounds.

21. I am myself unapologetically.

22. I am all the magic that I need.

23. All the validation I seek to thrive resides in me.

24. I let go of all the negative energies that pull me backwards.

25. I let go of all the insecurity I feel about myself.

26. I believe in my own power and ideas.

27. I am in a loving relationship with myself.

28. I'll not let what people think of me steal my joy.

29. I discard every hatred I have ever felt for myself.

30. I live my life graciously.

31. I become more beautiful with the break of every dawn.

32. I'll not destroy myself with hate and negativity. I am exceedingly kind to myself.

33. I forgive myself for all the times I looked down on myself.

34. I open my eyes to see all the awesomeness that lives in me.

35. I trust in my ability to take great care of myself.

36. I love myself deeply everyday.

37. I adore my body with everything in me.

38. My physical appearance isn't all the beauty there is to me. I am even more beautiful on the inside.

39. I am not overwhelmed by people's perception of me.

40. I radiate so much black excellence.

Key Points

My dear black woman, I hope these self-acceptance affirmations filled you with so much love and goodness. Remember everyday that you are the standard, and that you are the finest shade of black. I have curated amazing key points for this section just for you.

- You are the perfect definition of black excellence.
- No one's definition of you matters but yours.
- You are flawed and perfect all at once.
- Accept yourself in every way, and you'd see all the greatness that you bear.
- You are full of beauty.

I Am The Truest Fashionista Ever; Black Women Fashion Affirmations

I remember meeting this black woman at a party. She had this shiny skin that could pass for a new mirror. She's one of the most beautiful black women I've seen all my life. But thinking about her now, I wonder if she ever realized how beautiful she was. How much power the stare in her eyes possessed.

I remember that black woman and the discomfort on her face when she danced. She wore this flowing English dress that seemed to stifle her smile. I could tell that she wasn't comfortable in that dress at first glance. I wondered if anyone influenced her into wearing the dress. But I can't tell because I had no conversation with her. I was just an admirer admiring her gorgeousness from a distance.

A lot of black women have been ridiculed for dressing the way they do. If there's something a black woman pays a lot of attention to, it is her dress. Black women do not wear clothes simply because they want to cover up. They wear clothes to express themselves, tell their stories and live their truths. None of the black women I know loves to dress vicariously through anyone. They rather dress for themselves. But this is sadly difficult sometimes because some people have embarked on a mission to make black women feel bad for dressing the way they love. You'd find this behavior almost everywhere. In the office space, the churches, even at parties. It is that bad.

If black women continue to give in to the demands of people who want them to quit showcasing black excellence through their fashion sense, we might be heading towards a fashion era that is devoid of black women fashion in every way. That would be very terrible. Once a race begins to lose the major things that differentiates it from others, it would begin to head towards extinction. But I trust in the power of black women and black excellence not to allow this to become reality. Black is the color of power, black is culture, and culture must thrive. We don't thrive by mere words of mouth, we thrive much more by taking action.

I write these black women fashion affirmations for this reason. To strengthen all black women, make them appreciate the wonders of black fashion, and encourage them to embrace their own fashion styles. Don't look at me with confusion and anger yet, dear black women. I understand that it is not an easy thing to do. I also know that you possess all the power you need to do these. But I'm not letting you do all of it alone. I'll help you through the whole process by holding your hands and filling you up with positivity through it all like I have always done. Shall we begin?

Fashion Affirmations For The Black Woman

1. I make every dress perfect.
2. I wear my culture on my clothes.
3. I uphold black excellence through every piece of clothing that I wear.
4. My fashion sense makes me stand out from every crowd.
5. I have perfect skin that compliments my outfit.
6. I am blessed to be a black woman.
7. I have the truest fashion sense ever.
8. Beauty knows me by my name.
9. My foremothers dance in glee when I dress like the black woman that I am.

10. I'll have no one intimidate me into wearing clothes that I do not fancy.

11. I am very elegant.

12. My skin is an embodiment of the brightest stars.

13. My thick hair is the standard.

14. My fashion styles determine the trends.

15. I make the atmosphere joyful with the brightness of my clothes.

16. I am beyond beautiful. In fact, beautiful is a weak word to describe me.

17. I rock my styles with so much panache.

18. All heads turn to have a second at me when I walk past.

19. Fashion homes model designs after my styles.

20. I give fashion a newer and prettier meaning.

21. I portray black excellence with everything that I do.

22. My fashion style opens doors for me.

23. My fashion sense tells the stories of a generation of great women.
24. I am not consumed by society's idea of fashion.
25. I create my styles with ease.
26. If elegance were human, it would be me.
27. My body makes clothes into perfection.
28. Everything I wear turns out perfect on me.
29. My fashion style takes me to my roots.
30. I am as fashionable as I can be and that is the most important thing.
31. I am not afraid to dress the way I desire.

Key Points

My gorgeous black woman, I hope these fashion affirmations help you in finding the road that leads home. Home, where the trueness of black women's fashion resides. Below are the key points for this session.

- Your fashion sense tells the stories of generations of black women who knew and embraced black fashion in all its forms.
- It is okay to stand out all by yourself.
- Your fashion styles set new paces for fashion homes.
- Do not give anyone the permission to intimidate you into wearing clothes that you do not love.
- You are elegance in all its forms.
- You have a perfect body that makes every dress you wear perfect.

A lot of black women are ridiculed for the hair texture and skin type that they possess. Some of these black women have been made to believe the fallacy that their skin is not pretty enough and that their hair is bad. Since when did thick, full and bouncy afros become bad? When people do not understand a thing, they try to destroy it. This is the thing that people try to do to black women. They do not understand all that melanin and kinky hair. They are such a beautiful pair that people wonder the mystery behind that kind of beauty. But instead of admiring it, they'd rather ridicule it openly and envy it in secret. When you understand this simple logic, you'd begin to understand all the hate that is shown to black women because of their hair and skins.

Isn't it ironic how afro themed hair care and skincare products sell out quickly in the stores? Have you not wondered about this before? Who are the people purchasing these products if afro is as ugly and classless as some people try to make it seem? This should send a message home. Melanin is the truth and kinky hair defines class. Trust me, I do not say these to you to make you feel good about yourself or boost your self-confidence in any form. I am simply telling you the truth that has always been hidden from you. I understand that you might have gone through so much trouble and bad treatment for rocking your skin and your hair. That might make you believe that your afro isn't all that worth it. To love your hair and skin wholly, you would need to embrace everything about the black excellence. Doing this isn't very easy because of everything that society has portrayed about black women's beauty. But it is an achievable thing. My friend, I'm not asking that you do everything at once. Not at all, it is a gradual process. Begin by first dissociating yourself from the lies and malicious talks. Then you go further by falling in love all over again with your skin and your hair. Appreciate the beauty of that glossy skin and its softness. Then you admire that gorgeous forest that grows on your head. You don't have to worry so much about doing it all alone because I am always with you to help and guide you as you navigate your beauty with ease and joy. I write every affirmation in this session just for you. Hold my hand and let us call gorgeousness into you. Shall we begin?

1. I love my melanin and how it differentiates me from the crowd.
2. My hair is a crown of beauty.
3. I love my skin and how it glows.
4. My hair is soft and free from breakages.

5. My hair grows from beauty to beauty
   with each passing day.

6. I do not allow anyone to intimidate me
   for being uniquely beautiful.

7. My skin tone and hair texture are
   dreams.

8. I afford the right diets my hair and skin
   needs with ease.

9. I create enough time to care for my hair
   and skin.

10. I choose the best products for myself
    with elegance.

11. My complexion is so amazing.

12. My hair resists breakages and
    dandruffs.

13. I embrace my birth marks with joy.

14. I accept my skin with all of its
    perfections and imperfections.

15. I absolutely adore my hair.

16. I style my hair in the most classy ways.

17. I manage my hair with ease.

18. I am proud of my hair type and texture.

19. I get good value from all the money I spend on grooming my hair and nourishing my skin.
20. My skin is strong and powerful.
21. I derive pleasure in caring for my skin and hair.
22. My skin glows like the sun.
23. I am grateful for the gorgeousness of my skin.
24. I am confident in my skin and hair.
25. I am as classy as I can be.
26. I celebrate my perfect hair and skin.

Key Points

You know a black woman from the uniquely gorgeous texture of her hair and the silky nature of her skin. A black woman's hair and skin contain so much beauty that some people try to make themselves feel good by ridiculing her. It is high time this behavior stopped! I have curated the key points for this section that celebrates black women's excellent hair and skins.

- You are flawlessly beautiful.
- Your hair and skin add so much to your beauty.
- Discard all the lies that you were once made to believe about black excellence.
- Glow with pride. Suns like you do not thrive in hiding.
- Remember that you are as classy as you can be.

Again, we come to the end of a chapter. Tell me, did you have fun exploring these beauty and fashion affirmations? Do you feel more powerful now? Have you decided to step into your powers? Black women are so powerful. I do not want you to neglect your own powers. Make everything you do count. Do things the way you want them done. This is your one life. Be audacious!

We'll begin a new affirmation journey in the next chapter. We'll explore joy and its goodness! Come with me, let's speak joy into our wonderful lives.

Chapter Six

Joy Affirmations For The Black Woman

We cannot cure the world of sorrows, but we can choose to live in Joy.
—Joseph Campbell.

Life is filled with a lot of stress and trouble that one needs to work hard at one's happiness. Joy is one of the greatest emotions I know. Many people have defined joy in various contexts. Some say it is the state of being happy and content with all that there is around you. Others say it is happiness. For me, joy is more than just feeling. It is that light that floods your life and illuminates every darkness. It is that warmth that shields you from life's coldness. It is that fresh spring flower that blooms with ease and a lot of beauty.

Sometimes, we tend to think that joy is a special package that comes with a perfect life. But I put it to you that it is a fallacy. If joy was present only to people with perfect lives, no one on this green earth would know joy. Every life has its own lows and highs. Moments of despair and moments of exceeding hope. Memorable and regrettable moments. Do you see that joy is not reserved for a special class of people? It is one of life's beauties that goes into anywhere it is welcomed. Yes, you invite joy into your life. You create your own joy. Joy begins to trickle into your being the moment that you realize that you have the power to create it as you want. Yes, it is trickling into your being right now because you have come into the realization.

No one can possibly cleanse the world of all the sadness that clings to it. But it is possible to live in joy despite all that happens in the world. No, I am not asking you to be oblivious of reality. Rather, I am asking you to focus on making your life out to be one that welcomes joy. You might think you are undeserving of joy when you let the world's idea of 'a perfect life' overshadow your reason. You don't need perfection to welcome joy. Joy and perfection are two different entities. Remember this always. That things are not going as planned for you is no reason to deny yourself of joy. In fact, joy has a way of making you stronger. Joy opens your heart up to hope. And when hope comes, you get the strength that you need to try again. Tell me, don't you want to taste joy? I bet you do. When you find joy, you'd never want to let it go. I tell you this from my own experience.

Now, you might wonder how to welcome this joy that I speak so keenly of into your life. Joy is no tax collector, so you don't have to worry about paying a price for it. All you have to do is welcome it into your life and it will be all yours.

You can begin by stripping yourself of all the negativities that steal your joy. Be kind to yourself. You know, you are the biggest cheerleader you could ever have. Then you unlearn all the bad definitions of joy that the world made you believe at some point in your life.

Tell yourself that you are deserving of joy. Embrace your present life and work on an improvement with glee and not hate. Slowly, steadily, joy will build an amazing residence in you. I know you really want this joy. You'll get it.

My dear, I won't leave you alone to create your joy all by yourself. I'll hold you up like I have always done through the other chapters. I'll guide you through affirmations that will lead you into creating an endless flow of joy. Shall we begin?

I Begin My Day With Joy

This section is all about joy affirmations curated specially to bless your morning. You know, morning is a very powerful part of the day. It is in the morning that you make plans and decide how you want your whole day to turn out. This is why you should never take your morning lightly. Now, dig into these joy affirmations for your morning!

1. I invite joy in all its wholeness into my life this morning.
2. Joy rises into my life brightly like the morning sun.
3. Joy dwells in me from this morning until the end.
4. My joy is not a one time thing. It lasts for a long time.
5. I find joy in everything.
6. I give no one or anything the permission to take my joy away from me.

7. I spread joy and positivity to everyone I come across.

8. I am more than ready to carry joy.

9. I strip myself of everything that would make it impossible for me to have joy.

10. I choose joy today.

11. I am strengthened by joy.

12. I am exceedingly joyful despite the negativities around me.

13. I have made peace with the fact that I can't end the sadness in the world. I also come into the realization that I have all the power I need to create my own joy.

14. I step into my joy with ease.

15. The joy in me is so great that all the world sees it.

16. I do not allow the world to steal my joy.

17. My smile bears joy.

18. My morning is blessed with so much joy.

19. I give no room to sorrow.

20. I am joyful from the inside.

21. I wake into joy!

Key Points

Your day would turn out much greater and happier when you speak joy into it. That's why I encourage you to take morning affirmations for joy seriously. Below are the key points for this session.

- You have all the power you need to create a joyful day for yourself.
- Choose joy in the morning, and joy will cling to you.
- Joy strengthens.

I Choose Joy Above All Things

Many things in this life are subject to our choices. You have the power to make choices and decisions for yourself. But, some options seem to have more power over others. Don't get confused, black woman. I'll explain what I mean here to you in very clear terms with a very short story.

I remember this Tuesday in Spring a couple of years ago. I don't know why I find it difficult to recall the exact year it was. Well, not remembering the year won't affect the story in any way. So, I'll go on with my narration. That Tuesday remains one of the most remembered days in my life to this day. I had woken up early to get to work in time that morning. I had so much work on my desk that I wondered how I was going to fix it all. Not like worrying about it made any difference, I just couldn't help it. I used to worry a lot.

I got to work early enough and started my work for the day. Not without exchanging greetings with my colleagues of course. Everything was going fine until my boss arrived at the office two hours later. I knew something was wrong the moment he arrived because of his unusual sternness. My boss was usually an easy going and kind man. He was always cheerful too. He also had this permanent smile on his face. But on this Tuesday morning, the smile lost its permanence. He wasn't smiling at all. The atmosphere in our large office was so tense. It was so silent that we could almost hear ourselves breathe. It was scary. No one had any clue what the problem with our boss was, so we all decided to let sleeping dogs lie by just doing our work more carefully and being faster at it. That worked for a very short while. We were too troubled to even work as efficiently as we used to. That's the thing with tension. It has the power to make the fastest person into a snail.

I was quite close to my boss. Not the boss-staff relationship. It was more like a cordial friendship. I respected his boundaries even with the closeness. It was this closeness that made me decide to ask him what the problem was with all boldness. But before the words could form in my mouth, he dismissed me with a languid wave of his right hand. It was at that point I knew that whatever it was that stole his smile and made him behave in such a manner was a very serious thing. How right I was. Nothing on earth could have prepared me for what followed.

The suspense in the office was finally lifted when my boss called me to a private space and offered me a sack letter for no reason. He said my services were no longer needed at the firm. For a moment, I thought it was a big fat joke. I couldn't believe it. I was one of the best workers in the firm, so I couldn't even figure out the rationale behind the sack. That hurt me the most. My boss paid no attention to my tears. He wouldn't tell me why I got sacked either. That was the part that hurt me the most. I really wanted that closure. But he wouldn't give it. And there was nothing I could do about it.

When I finally accepted that my job was over, I hung around the environment hoping that he would call me back and say it was all a mix up. Oh, how I wished and cried for that. Sadly, it never happened. The whole incident threw me into serious depression. I felt like my life was over. It was just too much for me to bear. Also, being sacked without a reason made it harder for me. I spent two weeks gloating and contemplating suicide. My mental health was a big mess. Exactly three weeks after I lost the job, I sat my ass down and talked to myself for a long time. I made myself realize that gloating and wallowing in my depression could do nothing. It was on that day that I chose joy. Yes, joy is a choice that you alone have to make for yourself. Know this.

Now, let's go back to what I said about some options being more powerful than others now. Getting depressed was the more powerful option. It was the easiest thing to do in that situation. It would have taken so much strength for me to choose joy on that first day. This is why I say choosing joy can be difficult sometimes. But it is always worth it, believe me. The strength that came with choosing joy helped me apply for better jobs. In the end, I got a better one. I did not share this story to inspire you or something, I shared it to make you realize the power of choosing joy above all things.

This section is all about choosing joy no matter what. I wrote these affirmations just for you.

You too should learn to choose joy, always.
So, let's begin to affirm!

1. I choose joy no matter the situation.
2. Unfavourable circumstances won't steal my joy.
3. All the pains I have gone through do not define my story.
4. I am the most joyful soul I know.
5. I forgive myself for all the times I made myself suffer.
6. I choose joy even in difficult situations.
7. Everything turns into joy for me
8. I am not weighed down by obstacles.
9. My obstacles are stairs that lead me to higher heights.
10. I'll know joy all the days of my life.
11. I choose joy even when it seems crazy.
12. I am not consumed by sorrow.
13. I stand firmly on the strength that joy gives to me.

14. I am exceedingly joyful about my existence.

15. I distance myself from melancholy and its troubles.

16. I am aware that life isn't all rosy, so I won't crush my joy by expecting greatness in everything.

17. I am the chief creator of my joy.

18. There is so much joy within me.

19. I distance myself from killjoys.

20. I find help with ease when I get depressed.

21. Joy surrounds me on every side.

Key Points

Sometimes, life will present you with very tough situations that'll dissuade you from choosing joy. If you keep on waiting for things to eventually get better before you choose joy, you might have to wait for a very long time. It is for this reason that I urge you to choose joy at

all times. Below are the key points for this
session.

- You are the chief creator of your joy.
- Forgive yourself for all the times you chose sorrow and let joy flow into you.
- Do not let bad situations steal your joy.
- Do not wait for joy, choose it everyday, and it will come to you.

I Invite Joy Into My Being

If you wait for joy to come to you spontaneously, you might have to wait for a very long time. This is because joy hardly comes like that. You have to do the choosing. Joy comes to you the moment you choose it. The moment you open up your arms to it. Sometimes, people would wait for a lifetime in search of joy and end up not finding it. What mystery that would be! So, I am letting you know today that joy clings to whoever invites it. Don't spend so much time waiting for joy to find you of its own accord. Invite it into your being and it'll flourish there. Inviting joy into your being is one of the easiest things ever. It doesn't require your money and it doesn't make you sweat. You only have to make the decision. Then you open up your heart to it. That, my dear, is how to invite joy.

Invite joy into your life day. Also, open up your heart to the small and big things alike. It is an open heart that can find joy in places where other people can't. It is an open heart that can explore the essence of joy in all its forms. Again, you won't be inviting joy into your being all alone. I'll be holding your hand to lead you, guide you, and strengthen you as usual. Now, let us begin to invite joy into the whole of your being.

1. I open my heart up to joy.
2. I find joy even in the hidden places.
3. I do not struggle to find joy.
4. I burst forth with joy everyday.
5. I invite joy into my being with the break of every dawn.
6. I'll not wait all my life for joy to come to me. I choose it and I create it.
7. Joy clings to me everyday.
8. Joy flourishes in my heart everyday.
9. I am exceedingly joyful.
10. My joy lives until the end of time.
11. Joy knows my name.

12. I attract joy.

13. I spread joy wherever I go.

14. I am surrounded by joy.

15. Joy comes to me easily.

16. Joy blooms in my heart and soul.

17. I choose joy.

18. I am empowered by joy.

19. I do not regret choosing joy.

20. I open every part of me to joy.

Key Points

- You'll find joy when you open your heart to it and invite it into your being.
- Life is much more beautiful with joy in it.
- Choose joy everyday. It comes at no cost.

Now, we have come to the end of this chapter with joy. Tell me, gorgeous soul, does your heart leap in joy? Does your soul burst forth with joy? I believe it does. Life bears so much grief that living without joy is one of the saddest things ever. For every part of your life, choose joy, create joy, spread joy and live joyfully. Embrace these affirmations wholly and you'd find your own joy clinging to you.

A new chapter begins again. This time, we explore affirmations for independence. Independence is one of the greatest attires that one can wear. And that is why I will adorn you with it in the next chapter. Come along with me!

Chapter Seven

Affirmations for Independence for The Black Woman

I always did something I was a little ready not to do. I think that's how you grow. When there's that moment of 'Wow, I'm not really sure I can do this', and you push through those moments, that's when you have a breakthrough.
—Marissa Mayer

Independence is one of the greatest things ever. We need independence to thrive in a competitive world like ours. You'd wonder, what is this independence all about? What is all this fuss about independence?

My friend, I understand that you might be so full of love and kindness that you'd expect the same measure from the world and everyone around you. I am sorry to disappoint you, but I must tell you this. There will come a time in your life when you would have to stand all by yourself, be your own cheerleader, pat yourself on the back and encourage yourself. There will be demanding times, but they won't stress you too much if you're rooted in independence already because you'd surely know how to take care of your affairs properly without any external influence. Do you see why I urge you to learn how to be independent now?

It's okay to be afraid and unsure. It's okay to detest failing, it's okay to cry. It's okay to fear what would become of you should you fail at this independence thing. You know what's not okay? Not trying. Yes, not striving for that independence is not okay. It is an essential thing. Before I could boldly stand on my own and say I was independent, it took me quite a long time. You know, I used to have this loving perspective of the world. I used to see the world as one big family where each and everyone of us was required to cheer the other on. I had good people around me, so I didn't see the flaw in my thinking. I only realized it when I stepped into unfamiliar grounds. Places that required me to stand all alone. It was then I realized that nobody owed me shit. Excuse my French, please. This is the one truth that you should know. I'm not asking you to hate people or not seek help when you can, I am only telling you that we are not entitled to people's kindness, warmth, love, money, compassion and other things that we tend to think we are entitled to. Of course, it is human behaviour to crave these things and give them back in return. But, this world is not all that black and white. Do you get it?

It Is for this reason that you must try your hardest to attain self-independence. Somehow, life is much easier when we are solely dependent on ourselves. We won't have to deal with the emotional baggage and trauma from depending on other people. A question is rising in your heart, isn't it? I can tell.

How does depending on other people cause us trouble? I'll answer this question with a very short story.

Two students are writing an exam together. These students are very close friends, so they share a lot of things together. One of the students studies hard, while the other doesn't. The hard-working student promises to help the lazy student pass the exam by helping him out in the examination hall.

Exam day comes, and for some weird reason, both students are made to make use of a different sitting arrangement as opposed to the one they were used to. Due to this, the hardworking student passes the exam with flying colors while the lazy student fails woefully.

Now, let's look at it this way. If both students had studied, the lazy one wouldn't have failed. He failed because he depended on someone else to pass the exams. This is just an example. Worse things have happened to people and are still happening because of the absence of Independence.

Walking the independence path is not an easy thing to do. But trust me, it is totally worth it. I won't leave you alone to walk the path of Independence all by yourself. I'll be holding your hand as always through these powerful independence affirmations written just for you. Let's begin, shall we?

1. I trust fully in my own abilities and strength.

2. I am not afraid to do all that it takes to stand firmly on my feet.

3. I am the greatest cheerleader I could ever wish for.

4. I am aware of my weak points, I have all it takes to turn them into strengths.

5. I take advantage of every opportunity to be more independent.

6. I do not allow privileges and kindness to get into my head so much that I forget my independence.

7. I love and treasure my independence with the whole of my heart.

8. I am blessed to be this independent.

9. I do not waiver when I have to do things by myself.

10. I flourish in my independence.

11. Being independent is the most beautiful thing that has ever happened to me.

12. I cut away everything that steals my independence.

13. I have all the courage I need to walk away from situations that threaten my independence.
14. I do not give anyone the power to crush my independence and my power.
15. I am totally in control of all that concerns me.
16. My opinion of myself is the best and greatest there would ever be.
17. I thrive more when I'm independent.

Key Points

Did you enjoy these independence affirmations, I trust you did. I have more in stock for you! Before I go on, take your time and savor the key points for this session.

- You have all it takes to be independent.
- You have all the courage you need to walk away from the people and the things that threaten your independence.

- You are the greatest cheerleader you could ever have.
- You have the power to turn your weaknesses to strengths.

I Am Financially Independent

Black women glow the most when they are financially independent. Depending on anyone for finances is very frustrating and limiting. You'd have to explain what every money you get goes into. You'd be afraid of spending money on the things that make your heart dance because your benefactor doesn't fancy them. You'd have to tame your desires and give up a lot of things. Also, you'd work your ass off to be able to enjoy a small amount of luxury.

Financial independence is every black woman's dream. A lot of black women have attained it, and more of them will. Financial independence is more than just being able to wear cool clothes and live in a decent home. Financial independence makes you live the kind of life that you desire. Not only that, it also helps you not to stick to limitations that you would have surpassed but for your finances.

A lot of people hold the belief that financial independence simply translates into very fat bank accounts. This is a little part of it, but there's still a lot more to it that you do not know yet. Having a fat bank account simply translates to you having money in just one place. I don't really fancy that. I love to spread my money across different profitable ventures. By this, I mean investments.

Investing money would generate more passive income. You know why I call it passive? It's because I do not have to work for it. I'd enjoy the dividends of my investment while my capital is still intact. What more wonderful thing could there be? Dear black woman, learn to invest money in stocks and good businesses. It is one of the best ways to emancipate yourself from poverty and the troubles that come with not having enough money. I need you to know one thing before you dabble into investments. You have to prepare yourself for losses just as you anticipate the huge dividends. You know, the market fluctuates sometimes. Also, investment is a risky venture like business is. But, it is a risk worth taking.

You might have to take a couple of classes to be able to understand how the financial market works. There are also available training sessions by professionals that you can consider. That is the price that you must pay one way or the other. Don't let this price discourage you at all. It is worth it.
Every day, I understand that nothing is truly free in this life. Save for the kindness that we get from people and other gifts, humans have to pay certain prices for things. If you understand this, it'll help you so much. Also, you wouldn't depend on people or blame them when you don't take action.

I understand the struggles that come with financial independence. But, don't worry too much about it. You won't go through it all alone. I'm with you as always to lead you through life changing affirmations for financial independence. Hold my hand, and let us begin.

Financial Independence Affirmations For The Black Woman

1. I attract wealth.
2. I am well equipped and fully ready to receive the wealth that I seek.
3. I manage my finances very well.
4. Money is a tool that'll help me reach my goals.
5. I invite money into my life.
6. I refrain from spending poorly with ease.
7. I am not consumed by my desire for money that I begin to seek it the wrong way.

8. I attract wealth.

9. I have rich and powerful ideas that lead me into wealth.

10. I invest my money in the most profitable ventures.

11. I am grateful for financial literacy.

12. I am blessed with an innovative mind that births millions.

13. I do not invest with greed.

14. I am confident of living my biggest financial dreams.

15. I connect with people that are interested in my financial growth.

16. I forgive myself for all the poor financial decisions I once made.

17. I am not ashamed to seek the financial expertise of experts when I get confused.

18. I have all it takes to improve my financial strength.

19. I distance myself from impulse buying and other negative habits that stop me from saving.

20. I value money and I handle it greatly.

21. I do not spend frivolously to impress anyone.

22. I get good dividends from my investment.

23. I make the most incredible financial decisions.

24. I'll become as rich as I have always dreamt no matter what

25. Wealthy looks really great on me.

26. I depend wholly on myself to rise into wealth.

27. I am happy because I know I am certainly going to reach the level of financial independence that I desire.

Key Points

My dear black woman, financial independence is not an empty dream. Do not let anyone discourage you at all. We believe that these affirmations would be of immense help to you. Before we proceed to the next session, do well to note the key points below.

- You have everything it takes to attain financial independence.
- You become richer when you eliminate bad spending habits like impulse buying.
- You can become as wealthy as you aspire to be.
- Your financial goals will become more attainable when you connect with people who share similar money dreams with you.
- Investing rightly can make you rich.

I Am Emotionally Independent

Emotional independence is one of the greatest types of Independence that any black woman could possibly know. Emotional independence is all about being able to exercise absolute control over your emotions and emotional life. To be honest with you, emotional independence is quite difficult for almost everyone because of how powerful our emotions could be. Emotional independence is difficult, but it is not impossible. Remember this always. It took me some time to learn how not to be easily influenced by my powerful emotions.

In the past, I used to ignore people who wronged me and treated me like I didn't matter because I didn't want to hurt their feelings. I used to be all sweet and kind to everyone. Even people who were mean to me were not left out. I was taken for granted because I was that perfect description of a good person. An angel. One major incident happened with a person I used to call friend before I realized what I was doing.

I used to have this person who I loved with all my heart. No, not romantic love. It was platonic affection. I would do everything I could to make this person happy and comfortable, but this person would never do the same for me. At first, I would make up silly excuses for this person's terrible behaviour towards me because I was really scared of accepting the glaring truth that reality had presented. It continued this way until I could no longer bear it. I connected all the pieces of the jigsaw puzzle together and I realized that this person was just a parasite who stayed around me to take advantage of my kindness. It was a very painful realization for me. I do not regret anything about it at all. Does it surprise you? I expected it to. That singular incident taught me a lot of emotional intelligence. The learning process was very painful, but it was worth it in the end. Mind you, it didn't rob me of my kind heart nor goodness. Rather, it opened my eyes to see that not everyone deserves it. I also learnt to keep my emotions in check. Being emotionally weak costs one too much. If you're not very careful, you could end up suffering a very serious breakdown.

My dear black woman, there is nothing cute about giving an arm for a person who wouldn't give a finger for you. Sometimes, our emotions overshadow our reason and make us turn blind to these things. One of the greatest forms of slavery ever is emotional slavery. It makes you sit in a room that shrinks you because you are too weak or afraid to leave. It keeps you in a toxic relationship because you feel you might never find a lover as passionate as your abuser. It makes you pile up excuses for people who treat you like a piece of dirt.

The list goes on and on. It never ends. But I know that you have all it takes to bring emotional dependence to an end in your own life. Like I said earlier, it is not an easy thing to do. But it is always worth it. You must understand that emotional independence is not a magical thing that happens just once. It is not the burst of a balloon. It takes time. Quality time. Emotional dependence is a psychological thing that sticks to a person like a tattoo. It doesn't go away at once. Little by little. You can begin the journey to emotional independence by cutting away every single thing that makes you dependent. You would need a good amount of will power to do this well. It is totally okay if you are unable to do it all at once. You can as well do it little by little. Take small and steady steps. When the small steps accumulate over time they become big steps. You know that, don't you?

When you begin your emotional independence journey, do not make the mistake of going back to the things you left behind because you 'miss' them. This is one terrible mistake that many people make. Doing it could ruin the whole detachment and independence process for you. You might have to begin all over again. To avoid this, do everything you can not to ever go back.

The journey to emotional independence is a very stressful one. But you won't go through the stress and rigors all alone. I'll hold your hands carefully and tightly while I lead you through some strengthening emotional independence affirmations written just for you. Shall we begin?

1. I am in control of my emotions.
2. I do not give my emotions the power to dictate my life.
3. I am not easily influenced by my emotions.
4. I reciprocate the energy I get from people with so much ease.
5. I forgive myself for all the times I allowed my emotions lord over me.
6. I am not consumed by my emotions.
7. I refuse to give my emotions the power to overshadow my reasoning.
8. I have made peace with my emotions, I do not live in denial of them.
9. I will not let toxicity into my space because of my emotions.
10. I cut myself off from everyone and everything that manipulate my emotions.
11. I open myself up to gain emotional independence with elegance and ease.
12. I will never put myself up for abuse because of my emotions.

13. I step away from emotional manipulators.
14. I thrive the most when I am in control of my emotions.
15. I have mastered the act of calmness even when I am in a bad place.
16. I do not suffer any emotional trouble.
17. I accept my emotional flaws and I am willing to work on them.
18. I am powerful enough to do all it takes to gain emotional independence.
19. I accept that emotional independence is a process. I am willing to go through it all.

Key Points

My gorgeous black woman, remind yourself everyday of the power you possess. You have every single thing it takes to gain independence in every area of your life. Your

emotions are inclusive. Below are the key
points for this section.

- You have all it takes to become
  emotionally independent.
- Emotional independence is a process, it
  is not a one time thing.
- Everything could become a mess if you
  let your emotions overshadow your
  reason.
- Accept your emotional flaws and work
  on them.

I Make The Best Decisions All By Myself

Decision making is one very important aspect of our lives. It takes quite a lot to make good decisions. A lot of people find it hard to make their own decisions. Does this surprise you? People can still make decisions without necessarily knowing what decision making is all about. Some people also make their own decisions by consulting other people and finding out what they think about the decisions they are considering. This is actually a nice thing to do. One would make better decisions if one consults with the right people. This behavior only becomes a problem when the individual is unable to make independent decisions.

Independent decision making is all about being able to make good and wise decisions without the interference of other people. You know, at some point in your life, you would have to make decisions. Some of these decisions would require urgency. A bad decision is capable of ruining a lot of things for you and the ones you love. In a case of urgency where your yes or no could fix or mar things, who would you first consult before taking action? Yourself. The earlier you learn this, the better for you. You have to master the act of independent decision making. You'll never regret it.

Just like emotional independence, independent decision making might take you a while to fully master and practice. This is simply because habits die hard. Especially habits like this one that become a part of us. But, it is not impossible. No matter how dependent you are on other people when you need to make your decisions, you can still become independent. It only takes time.

The first step that you should employ as you begin to master independent decision making is acknowledgement. You have to acknowledge your dependence and inability to make your own decisions at that point in time. Living in denial of it would do you no good, really. Acknowledgement is that big step that you must first take. Afterwards, speak to yourself from the depth of your heart. Remind yourself that you possess a great brain that can help you make great decisions. Of course, being intelligent isn't all there is to making good decisions. But, reminding yourself of that intelligence, versatility, open mind, rationality and other important factors would surely increase your self-confidence. Do you know why self-confidence is important in decision making? It helps you trust your own decisions. Sometimes, people don't trust their own decisions. This is not because those people are bad at making decisions, it is because they lack self-confidence when it comes to decision making. Such people would still be afraid even after making the best decisions in the world. It is for this reason that I urge you to be confident of your own intelligence and ability to independently make good decisions for yourself. You have to be in charge of every area of your own life.

At first, when you begin to make your own decisions, you would want to go back to the old style of consulting other people. It is a normal feeling. Don't let it bother you too much. Do not give in to it either. My friend, that is the thing with habits. But you have all the power that you need to fight it off. Whenever the feeling comes knocking at the doors of your heart, remind yourself yet again of the price you paid to get to that level. You did not go through a lot of thought and growth processes to fall back to dependent decision making just like that.

I understand that the journey to independent decision making is no easy one. But I am certain that you can win. I'll be with you to strengthen and guide you through the process by taking you through powerful affirmations for independent decision making. Hold my hand and let us begin. Shall we?

1. I trust in my ability to make great decisions independently.
2. I am not afraid to decide major things in my own life.
3. I embrace independent decision making with all of my heart.
4. I refuse to be irrational and overly emotional in my decision making.
5. I make good decisions with a lot of ease.
6. I am aware of the importance of independent decision making.
7. My decision making process is not influenced by unimportant things.

8. I do not feel guilt for the times I could not make my own decisions.

9. I make the best decisions concerning my own affairs.

10. I am not pressured into making decisions that are bad for me.

11. I have a very brilliant thought process.

12. My decisions matter the most in my own life.

13. I give no one the power to bully me into making decisions that I do not like.

14. I am full of wisdom, I apply my wisdom in my decision making.

15. I do not let anyone make me feel terrible for making the best decisions for myself.

16. My decisions are valid, I'll not change them to fit in people's expectations of me.

17. I do not depend on other people to make decisions for myself.

18. I make good decisions even within a short time frame.
19. I am at peace with the fact that not all my decisions would turn out the way I expect them to.
20. I respect the decisions of others.

Key Points

Independent decision making has become a necessary skill that every one should possess. I believe these affirmations would lead you gallantly into the beautiful world of independent decision making. Below are the key points for this session.

- You have all it takes to make good decisions independently.
- Do not feel guilt nor beat yourself up for all the times you depended on people to make good decisions.

- Independent decision making is a process. It is not a one time thing. Be patient with yourself.

Again, we have come to the end of a chapter. Did you enjoy these independence affirmations? I trust that you did. Before we go on to the next, I want to advise you to always employ these affirmations in your daily life. You'd be amazed at how much independence that you would gain.

The next chapter is all about healing. You know, no one thrives by carrying so much hurt around. Come along with me, we'll explore affirmations for healing in interesting ways in the next chapter. Shall we begin?

Chapter Eight

Healing Affirmations For The Black Woman

Instead of saying, I'm damaged, broken, and I have trust issues, say, I'm healing, rediscovering myself, and starting over.
—Horacio Jones

At some point in our lives, we go through pain. Some of these pain could be light. Light enough for us to heal from them very quickly. But some could be very deep. So deep that we begin to think healing is an impossible thing. But I'll remind you that healing is never impossible no matter what. The only truth is that healing requires a lot of courage. It takes courage to even accept that you are breaking apart, that you have embraced so much sorrow, that your heart bleeds.

Several years ago, I experienced one hell of a heartbreak. I felt like dying. My whole world became dark. I wished to die or at least become oblivious of all that pain. The pain bore deeply into my bones. I thought I would be miserable for the rest of my life. But, look at me now. Full of joy and so much love. Healing of any kind only begins when you are ready for it. When you open up your heart to it. Healing first begins with acceptance. You know, a lot of people feel disappointed in themselves when they go through certain situations. They'd feel weak and powerless. Some would feel like the most terrible people on earth, some would curse at the world's injustice and weep deeply about it.
In all of this, do not cause yourself more pain by living in denial of your hurt. You have to understand that it could have happened to

anyone. You also have to understand that these things don't happen because you are a bad person. They happen because they can. It is okay if you want to be a little hysterical before the acceptance. It is okay to cry and cuss at fate. But it is not okay to be at a low place forever. You know that, don't you?

My darling woman, I am urging you to drop that baggage of pain that continually steals your joy. No matter what happens, you are deserving of joy. And most importantly, healing. When you heal, joy will flow effortlessly. Healing is not wearing fake smiles in the midst of people and pretending it no longer hurts. Healing is all about embracing the hurt, letting go of it and not letting it decide your life anymore. You are a queen who is in charge of her own life. Pain is too small to influence your life till the end. No, I'm not trying to belittle your pain. Rather, I am letting you know that pain is unworthy of ruling your magnificent life. You deserve something great and beautiful and kind. Today, step into the path of healing and embrace it. Also, remember to walk away from all the things that break you. Don't worry, I won't let you walk the path alone. I'll hold your hand as always and walk you through powerful affirmations for healing. Believe me, you are going to heal. You are going to smile again. Now, shall we begin?

1. I welcome total healing into my existence.
2. I'll no longer allow the pain I experienced to rule my life.
3. I acknowledge the hurt and all that it brought, but I'll not wallow in them. I choose healing.
4. My past experiences do not define me.
5. I give nothing the power and the permission to steal my joy.
6. I am worthy of healing.

7. I believe in my ability to heal and be joyful again no matter the depth of the pain.
8. Healing comes easy to me.
9. I'll not pretend to have healed when I have not.
10. I understand that healing is but a gradual process. I am willing to go through all of it.
11. I believe in my unique ability to heal from every fall.
12. I am happy to heal.
13. I understand the essence of healing, I desire it with my heart. And I know that I'll get it no matter what.
14. I have all the courage I need to walk away from everything that breaks me.

Key Points

When pain is acknowledged, healing becomes much easier. This section is all about healing and rising above the pain. Find the key points for this session below.

- Healing begins to happen when you acknowledge the pain and decide to not let it govern you anymore.
- You have all it takes to heal.
- Be bold enough to walk away from all the things that cause your pain.
- Remind yourself always that healing is not an impossible thing to achieve.
- Nothing possesses the power to stop your own healing.
- You are in charge of your own life. Live it as such, my dear black woman.

Healing of The Body

Do you feel so much pain in your physical body that you wonder if it'll ever go away? Do you suffer from an illness? Does it hurt a lot? Does it break you from the inside?
I want you to know one thing. You'll find this healing that you seek, it will come to you, never to disappear ever again. Your body is not a home to illnesses. It is a home to good health, peace of mind and absolute love. You deserve a healthy body and all the goodness that heralds it. And you will get it. No, these are not just words. They will come to pass. Say them to yourself everyday with power.

While you make affirmations for good health in your body, please do not make the mistake of ignoring your medications because you are expecting some sort of miracle to happen. I have seen a lot of people do this. You know, they'd abandon their medications and begin to disobey their doctor's instructions. Healing doesn't work like that at all. It is one thing to acknowledge the illness and weakness in your body, it is also another thing to heal. Healing requires you to diligently take your medications. Your medications are like catalysts that trigger your healing. If you don't take them, how will healing come?

Also, a lot of people shy away from medications because of fear. This unexplainable fear of things going wrong or getting worse because of the medications. When people are like this, they'd subconsciously look out for stories of medicine killing people, infections making people paralyzed and other similar stories like these ones. I think this behavior is a human thing. Whenever we humans find a thing scary, we begin to look out for scarier things about that thing to reaffirm our stance.

My friend, that's a very toxic way to live life.
Doing that will make you blind to healing.
That's not the only thing it does. It also fills your
mind up with a lot of negativity. Negativity has
a great power. It weakens you beyond your
imagination. And, I am sure that's not what you
want for yourself. To know healing, you have to
master how to eliminate negativity. It slows
down healing. Going to good hospitals can
help reduce your fear. Do you know why? The
chances of facing complications and being
treated the wrong way is lesser in good
hospitals with qualified health care personnel
compared to substandard hospitals. The only
downside to it is that you would have to spend
more money on health care. The truth is,
quality health care is not cheap.

But, this won't be so much of a problem to you
if you have health insurance. Health insurance
companies work hard to help you get quality
health care at the cheapest prices. You should

consider getting one. You mustn't be ill before getting health insurance. In fact, it is a necessity. Don't let anyone tell you otherwise.

Choose healing and decide to see the best things. Think healing and embrace healing. You'd be surprised at the amount of healing that you'll know. Choosing healing is not very easy. No thanks to sad stories people hear and the pessimism that comes with being ill sometimes. None of these should discourage you. You have the power to not allow them. Remember this always. In this section, I'll hold your hands tightly like I have always done. Then I'll walk you through some wonderful affirmations for healing in your body. I write each and every one of them for you. I pour all my love in them. Now, let's begin your healing journey. Shall we?

1. I have good health in my life.
2. I acknowledge my pains, and I know they'll go away.
3. I do not give my illness the power to dictate my life.
4. I'll walk through this and leave unscathed.
5. This pain will not steal my joy.
6. Good health comes easy to me.
7. My medications work beautiful wonders in my body.
8. This pain will not be the end of me.
9. I eat healthy foods. I take off all unhealthy foods from my diet.
10. I am healthier and stronger than ever before.
11. My cells work towards healing. Every organ in my body is receptive of good health and strength.
12. I welcome happiness and peace and good health into my life.

13. I release all toxins and disease causing organisms from my body.
14. I do not take my medications in vain, they will work efficiently and help me heal fully.
15. I entertain thoughts of healing alone. Negative thinking has no place in my mind.
16. I have a very strong immune system that works to ensure that I am healthy.
17. I am encompassed by healing energies.
18. I have an amazing body.
19. I am grateful for good health.
20. I take care of my body.
21. I indulge in only healthy habits.
22. I release every negative emotion that is making me unhealthy.
23. My body gets every nutrient it requires from what I eat.
24. I am full of unstoppable energy.
25. I am very delighted to be alive.

26. I radiate positivity, strength and good health.

27. I develop a healthy lifestyle.

28. I am deserving of good health.

29. I am open to discarding everything that works against my health.

30. I love and adore my body. I forgive myself for the times I didn't care for my body well.

31. I am not overwhelmed by the pain and discomfort I feel.

Key Points

Good health is one of the greatest things anyone could ever have. That is why I am exceedingly glad that I led you through these powerful healing affirmations. Below are the key points for this section. Remember them daily, would you?

- You are deserving of good health.
- Your thoughts affect your health. Think and embrace positivity always.
- Love your body, nurture it like a tender child. Do not forget to forgive yourself for the times you didn't treat your body right.
- Healthy foods would help you heal faster. Ditch all the junk.
- You'll walk through your illness and leave unscathed.

My Heart Is Healed; Affirmations For Heartbreak

A heartbreak is one of the saddest things that could ever happen to anyone. It's sadder when you tried all you could to make it work and it never did . You'd cry and wonder where it all went wrong. You'd see pictures of your lover and cry your heart out. Your favorite memories might even begin to haunt you. For someone like me who has experienced a couple of heartbreaks, I understand how it steals one's happiness and makes one second guess every act of kindness. It is that terrible.

When the relationship is over, don't blame yourself for anything. It only worsens everything. I can attest to this. The first time my partner broke up with me, I contemplated suicide. It was my first relationship and I had wished it would end with a happily ever after. You know, I wanted a perfect love story where it's all rosy and sweet. When my partner sent me the breakup text, I felt like a part of me died. That is the thing with loving people. When you love anyone, especially in a romantic relationship, you give a part of yourself to that person. When the relationship ends, you'll try to get that part of yourself back. That's almost impossible. The hurt and detachment would literally ruin you. You'll find yourself breaking up at the slightest thing.

When that break up happened, I spent days gloating and wondering what went wrong. I kept on trying to find out what I did wrong. I still faulted myself even in situations where I did nothing wrong. I was desperately in love. I didn't even realize when I started apologizing for the things I didn't do. I did every single thing I could to make my partner take me back. But it was all futile. I desperately needed some closure, but my partner didn't give it. It made me think so much and wonder what I did wrong. I was blind to all the toxicity in the relationship. The verbal abuse and everything. I always felt like I wasn't enough. At some point, I began to do things I usually wouldn't do because I wanted to keep my partner. I didn't realize I tried too hard until it ended. A good number of black women stay put in toxic relationships because of the fear of losing their partners. It's one of the most toxic things ever. You are too full of beauty and intelligence to be treated like dirt. When the relationship begins to shrink you and shape you into what you do not like, do yourself some honor and catwalk away like the Queen that you are. It is not an easy thing to do, but it is worth it. It'll save you from future heartbreak.

Now, remember that the first step to take in order to heal is to accept the reality of the break up. Not like there's anything that you can do about it. Then, don't blame yourself for anything. Don't blame your partner either. It ended because you both wouldn't work out. Don't gloat about it. Also, don't hurt yourself by trying to live in denial. Pretending it never happened only makes the pain go deeper.

The mending of a broken heart is a very gradual process. On some days, you'd party and celebrate your healing. On other days, you fall into deep sadness because your favourite memory of your partner made you cry. You'd heal sometimes and relapse sometimes. But the ultimate truth is that you'd definitely heal no matter what. You have to take little and steady steps as you navigate your way around healing. You'll need a good amount of courage too. Then self-control. It is self-control that'll keep you from calling your ex at the slightest opportunity. It is courage that'll make you slowly discard the things that trigger your tears no matter how much those things used to mean to you. Do you understand this?

One more thing. Take as much time as you need to heal. Don't make the mistake of getting into a new relationship immediately because you want to prove a point to your former partner. It is a very dangerous game to play, and you'd be the only one that ends up hurt in it. You don't need to prove anything to your partner. Your healing and happiness is all that matters. Let this stick.

Don't fret, you won't walk through this healing alone. I am with you as always to lead you through sincere and beautiful healing affirmations. Your heart won't stay broken forever. Hold my hand and let us begin.

1. I am grateful for all the good times I had in my past relationship. I regret nothing at all.
2. This break-up is the beginning of a beautiful phase in my life.
3. I am happy to begin my life afresh.
4. I choose to be happy despite the hurt.
5. I am my own happiness.
6. I choose healthy relationships.
7. I love myself at all times.
8. I accept my hurt, and I'll do everything I can to heal from it.
9. I do not wish my former partner any pain.
10. There is so much love in me.
11. I am grateful to have loved and be loved.
12. I let go of the hurt.
13. I am not afraid to open my heart to love.
14. I know that I'll find the love I deserve someday.
15. I heal with elegance and ease.

16. I forgive myself.

17. My life is beautiful the way it is.

18. This heartbreak won't ruin my love life. I'll have a wonderful relationship with my new partner.

19. I'll never give up on who I am for the sake of a relationship.

20. I have all the courage I need to walk away from a toxic relationship.

21. I am grateful for the lessons my previous relationship taught me.

22. I attract my dream partner.

23. I believe in my ability to heal.

24. There is a better person waiting for me.

25. I do not give up on love.

26. My heart is whole.

27. I understand that healing takes time, I am ready to go through the process.

28. I'll love and laugh again.

29. I am worthy of love.

30. I am too beautiful to be stuck in a bad relationship. I walk away with all elegance.

Key Points

You'll heal from the heartbreak, you'll find your dream partner and you'll love again. Below are the key points for this session.

- You'll heal from the hurt.
- A failed relationship doesn't define your love life.
- Don't be afraid of walking out of a toxic relationship.
- You are worthy of love.
- You heal faster when you don't live in denial of your pain.
- You are whole.

Affirmations For Mental Healing

When we talk about good health, most of us just think about our physical body. But, that's not all there is to good health. Our mental health is one aspect of our health that we do not pay a lot of attention to. Mental health includes our psychological, emotional and social well-being. Anything that affects our mental health has the power to affect our physical body too. This is one great reason why we should never ignore our mental health.

There's this popular misconception that a lot of people hold about mental health. They think it doesn't just come, that it is always caused by something. No, this is not always the truth. Sometimes, one can begin to face mental health problems out of the blue. I'll use depression as an example. I used to think that I could never get depressed because of the great life I had. I mean, I live my life on my terms and I am able to do the things that I desire with a lot of ease. Why would I get depressed? I thought like this until a strong wave of depression hit me from nowhere. I began to lose interest even in those things that made my whole existence nearly perfect. At first, I lived in denial of it. I felt greatly disappointed in myself. What reason did I have to fall into depression?

I lived in my denial for a while. I had to get a therapist. It was that kind therapist that sat me down and educated me about mental illnesses and how they could happen to just anyone. I did a lot of unlearning, and I'm absolutely grateful for all of them. Now that I have talked about this misconception, I will talk about the triggers. Your triggers are simply the things that cause a fall in your mental health. Those things that cause mental illness. Triggers could be anything. They could be your own thoughts, people, memories, situations and a lot of others. Some people suffer a lot of mental health issues because they find it difficult to identify their triggers.

To have good mental health and to be able to recover from any mental illness quickly, you need to learn how to identify the things that cause your mental illness. Doing it all by yourself could be very stressful sometimes, so you can always do it with a therapist. Don't be ashamed to talk about what you go through with a therapist, it's one of the first and greatest steps that you can ever take towards true healing.

My dear black woman, you have to learn how to guard your mental health with jealousy. Guard it and treasure it with everything that you are. There's something I want you to know. You do not have to indulge anyone or anything that robs you of good mental health no matter how 'tempting' it appears to be. Nothing, my dear, is worth your mental health. If your mental health is unstable, it would affect a lot of things in your life. Not just your physical health, but other important things like your productivity, relationships, finances and a lot of others. Do you realize how important your mental health is now? Never trade it for anything. Whenever you notice that your mental health is unstable, do not ignore it. It could grow into something terrible. Get the help you need.

I know that walking this path of adequate mental health care is not an easy thing to do at all. But I know that you can do it. I trust in your abilities. All of them! I won't leave you alone to walk the path all alone. I'll be with you as always and hold your hands and walk you through some powerful mental health affirmations written just for you.

1. I take absolute charge of my mental health.
2. I am not ashamed to seek health for my mental issues.
3. I guard my mental health with jealousy.
4. Nothing is worth my mental health.
5. I have all the courage I need to walk away from anything that threatens my mental health.
6. I love and cherish my mental health.
7. I have all it takes to heal completely from mental illness.
8. I do not give my trauma the power to rule my life.
9. My mental illness doesn't define me. I am so much more.
10. I do not live in denial of my mental illness.
11. My mental health flourishes greatly.
12. I walk away from everything that triggers me with ease.

13. I do not keep my triggers close for any reason.
14. I am not ashamed nor afraid to open up to my therapist.
15. I have all I need to heal.
16. My mental healing is not an impossible thing, it'll come to me no matter what.
17. I break free from every single thing that torments my mental health.
18. I do not entertain anything that affects my mental health.
19. I have access to the kind of therapy that I need.
20. I have the finances I need to take care o of my mental health.
21. I do not ignore my mental health.
22. I am not afraid to dissociate myself from anyone that makes me fall into depression.
23. I do not blame myself for my mental illness.

24. I am aware that a mental illness is not a death sentence, I'll heal and be joyful again.

25. I do the things that make me joyful.

Key Points

Embrace mental healing as much as you embrace physical healing and you'd see how well you would function. Below are the key points for this section.

- Your mental health is worth it. Do not keep your triggers close.
- Do not be ashamed of getting help, getting help doesn't make you weak.
- Be strong enough to walk away from everything that makes a mess of your mental health.
- A mental illness is not a death sentence, you'll heal, and you'll be joyful again.

We have come to the end of this chapter! It was such a beautiful and heartwarming thing to go through these affirmations with you. I hope these healing affirmations strengthen you and help you heal in the most beautiful ways. The next chapter is all about affirmations for black women in leadership. It promises to be a very rewarding chapter. Read on, let's explore it all together!

Chapter Nine

Affirmations For Black Women In Leadership

Leadership is not about titles, positions and flowcharts. It is about one life influencing another.
—John Maxwell

Whenever leadership is mentioned, most people tend to only think of being in the position of power. You know, all that authority and power. The titles and the privileges that come with position. But, leadership is beyond that. John Maxwell reaffirms in the quote I wrote at the beginning of this chapter. To be a leader is to oversee the affairs of a certain group. To be a leader is to ensure that everything about that group tilts towards the right direction. Leadership involves a lot of management and care more than it involves the use of power. This is why passion and dedication are one of the major attributes of good leaders. If a leader has no passion for the office, the leader may not be able to do a very good job.

Black women make great leaders. Black women are strong, resilient, powerful and full of intelligence. Believe me when I tell you that black women are one of the most intelligent people on earth. This might cause a question to brew in your heart. Why then do black women shy away from contesting for offices? There are a lot of reasons for this. Some black women shy away from power because they believe the false narrative other people sold to them about black women not being good enough to occupy positions of power. This is one big lie that some black women have been made to believe. If you believe in this lie, I put it to you that it is a fallacy. Take it out of your heart today and thrash it. It holds no atom of truth.

There are also black women who do not contest for offices because of fear. The fear of not being able to do it right. Leadership is very overwhelming, but you can do it awesomely if you put your heart to it. You have the unique ability to do anything you desire if you put your heart to it. Yes, you are powerful like that. Letting fear govern your desire for leadership would make you unable to reach your potential. I understand your fears. Your fears are valid. But your fears become very strong when you give it power. You give your fear power when you let it take deep roots in your life. When you let it determine the outcome of your life. My dear black woman, don't you want an adventurous, beautiful and fulfilling life? I know you do for sure. It is very achievable. But how can you achieve it with fear? How can you step out of conformity if you are afraid? No way at all. You have to kill that fear.

Look around you today. There are lots of black women doing great things in leadership. For them, I'll write the affirmations in this session. A lot of black women agitate for revolution. But only few black women are willing to do what it takes to bring the revolution. These women are found in leadership. Are you a black woman in leadership? Does it get overwhelming sometimes? I know it does. But you can win no matter what. You can leave your mark in this world of ours.

I understand how overwhelming being in the leadership sector is, but I urge you not to throw in the towel. I am right there with you to encourage you, cheer you on and strengthen you. Hold my hand and let us walk through some powerful affirmations for black women in leadership together.

1. I do absolutely well in leadership.

2. I have all it takes to be a leader.

3. I embrace quality leadership only, mediocrity does not thrive in my space.

4. I am willing to lead other black women like me into the revolution that they seek.

5. I thrive in leadership.

6. I am no despotic leader, I lead with kindness, love and fairness.

7. I care about the opinions of my followers.

8. I incorporate true democracy into my leadership.

9. I am the best leader there is.

10. I am not overwhelmed by the difficulties that come with leadership.

11. I am deeply loved and valued by my followers.

12. I am not afraid to stand for what is right.

13. I am not afraid to stand up to oppressors.

14. I give leadership a more beautiful and brighter meaning by being a very good leader.
15. I make decisions that favor my followers and every single person under my leadership.
16. I am not afraid to lead.
17. I am blessed with enlightened and understanding followers.
18. Leadership is not a struggle for me.
19. I lead with passion, I am not blinded by the power that comes with my position.
20. I do not intimidate my followers into obedience. I make them see reasons with me instead.
21. I am grateful for being able to lead.
22. I value my followers greatly.
23. I am the best version of myself even in leadership.

Key Points

Dear black woman, I hope these affirmations help you in your quest to become a great leader. Below are the key points for this section.

- You have all it takes to lead.
- The opinions of your followers matter. Do not impose anything on them.
- Do not be blinded by the power that comes with leadership. It could ruin you.
- Be fair and honest in your leadership.
- Believe in your dreams and vision, do not let anyone intimidate you into silence.

Affirmations For Black Women Looking To Venture Into Leadership

A lot of black women do not venture into leadership because they do not get the push they need. Some people love to be motivated into action. While others just do their thing all by themselves. The first group of people are larger in population than the second group. There is no difficult science behind this. When people motivate you, you'll feel this sense of support and love. You'll know that you're not alone. The truth is, when we are pursuing anything, we tend to give more energy to it when we know that people are solidly behind us. For a thing like politics where winning or losing is a major thing, we'd desire more motivation and support than ever.

But what happens if there is no one to support us the way we want to be supported? What becomes of our ambitions if the only support we have is ourselves? Do we abandon them or do we forge ahead? Abandoning them looks like the easiest thing to do, right? It is, but it isn't. Abandoning your ambitions because you did not find the support you need is not a great thing to do. You'll end up hurt and sad in the long run. You may hate yourself for not trying at all. Believe me, regret is one of the worst feelings ever. It'll make you beat yourself up and hate yourself. The powerlessness of it all is even more terrible because you won't be able to do anything to erase the past. Traveling back in time is the perfect thing to do, but it exists only in the world of fiction. This is real life, dear woman. You have to know that you are all the motivation that you need. Your support and love for yourself will take you far. When people see you excelling and moving mountains all by yourself, they'll be interested in joining your cause. Success has many friends is no cliché at all. It indeed has many friends. That's why people would fight against a cause at first and later support it because they want to identify with success.

I believe you have your answer now. Don't you? If you're in search of motivation or a push, look deeply within yourself and you'll find all that you seek. The passion that you have for what you do will motivate you. Your big dreams will motivate you. The goals of your leadership will motivate you. Leadership mostly comes with a lot of opposition. You have to get ready for them. Don't expect everyone to welcome you with open arms or smile with you. All you really have is you. Your supporters come second. You're curious about why this is so right? See, you may treat people with all the kindness and love that you know and still have them treat you like shit. Naturally, you would expect people to treat you the way you treat them, right? I used to think like that too. But I have long learnt that the world doesn't work like that. People won't always treat you the way you would treat them and things won't always go the way you plan. Know this and know peace.

Also, don't try to get into leadership by buying your way through people's hearts and bringing out your true self later. It doesn't end well. Not only do you break people's trust, you also teach them not to support you later. Don't make the mistake of wearing a mask to be loved, be your most authentic self. The people that will love you will love you and the ones that will support you will. Pretence is a dangerous game to play.

Don't be afraid to go into leadership, you can win big if you work towards it. I understand that leadership is no stroll in the park too. That is why I'll be giving you all my love and support.

I'll hold your hand through every line in this section and walk you through powerful affirmations I specially wrote for every black woman who is looking to go into leadership.

1. I have all it takes to lead.
2. I am my biggest supporter.
3. I am willing to learn all that there is to becoming a good leader.
4. I'll do exceedingly great in leadership.
5. I'll not become who I am not to be loved by people. I'll be my most authentic self.
6. I am proud to be in leadership.
7. I am not afraid to go into leadership.
8. I'll achieve all of my leadership dreams.
9. I don't gloat over poor leadership, I'll go into it and change the narrative.
10. I am the dream of black women leadership.
11. I'll win on every side.
12. Leadership comes easy to me.

13. I am governed by my passion and love for leadership.

14. I am deeply loved and supported.

15. I lead with wisdom and confidence.

16. I am not afraid to lead.

17. I trust in my leadership skills.

18. I open myself to learning things that would make me a good leader.

19. I am not consumed by leadership.

20. I am a wonderful leader.

21. I have all it takes to be the kind of leader I have always dreamed of.

22. I'll perform more than my expectations.

23. I am ready to give my best to leadership. I'll not be blinded by power or money.

24. I understand that leadership is more than just office work. I'll be the leader that works above it.

Key Points

My dear black woman, do not be afraid to go into leadership. You have everything it takes to do it excellently. Below are the key points for this section.

- You have everything you need to become a leader.
- Do not let the wealth or power that comes with your office stop you from executing your dreams.
- Open yourself to learning all the time. It'll make you a good leader.
- Don't complain so much about the state of leadership, go into it and change the narrative to a better one.

Affirmations For Black Women Being Intimidated In Leadership.

A lot of black women have conquered many obstacles surrounding black women leadership. A lot of black women have risen into leadership. One would think this is all there is not knowing there is more in store. I used to think that every other obstacle would cease to exist the moment black women debuted into leadership. I was so wrong. It is saddening that a lot of black women still face problems while in leadership. The most common problem that they face is intimidation. Does this amaze you? It doesn't amaze me so much, really. People are greatly threatened and frightened by the enormous power and audacity that black women show in leadership. So they try to silence black women by intimidating them into silence. I'm not making this up. Engage black women in leadership in deep conversations and you'll be amazed at how much this intimidation has eaten deep into black women leadership. But I beg of you, do not let it deter you. Black women come from a history of Amazons and great women who trampled anything that tried to kill them to death. No one can end the power of a black woman unless she gives that person permission. Are you awed by this? Don't be. It is the truth about you. This is the truth that they do not want you to know. They do not want you to know it because the more self-aware you become, the more difficult it would be to intimidate you.

How can black women deal with the issue of intimidation in leadership? Do they back out or not? Giving up is never the option in cases like this one. Running away from a bully empowers the bully to trouble you more. You fight a bully by standing up for yourself. In high school, I had a bully in my class. He'd torment us, forcefully take our snacks and force us to do his school work for him. We'd do everything he commanded because we were afraid of being intimidated and beaten. None of us ever dared to speak up. Our silence empowered the bully. The bullying continued until I could no longer bear it. I had to become the Devil's Advocate. I reported to our teacher. Our teacher dealt seriously with the bully and the bullying stopped for a while. It started again. This time, I was the only target of the bully. My crime was reporting to the teacher. The bully made life so much hell. At that point, I realized that reporting to the teacher wasn't the best solution. I had to fight for myself. There comes a point in your life where you would have to stand up for yourself. It was that point in my own life. It met me afraid and without preparation.

One day, I got into a fist fight with the bully. I don't know what gave me that courage till this day. Before anyone could stop us, I had beaten the bully to a pulp. I cried in amazement. I never knew I could win such a bulky frame in a fight. It was too good to be true. That fight caused a turning point in my life. I humbled the bully.

Most people that intimidate black women in leadership are like this bully. Their weapons are always fear, intimidation and the manipulation of power to suit selfish interests. My dear black woman, I urge you to stand up for yourself and fight them off like my younger self. You don't know how powerful you can be until you try. If you're too afraid to fight all alone, tell your sisters, other black women like you. When black women unite, they become invincible.

I won't leave you to fight the intimidation all alone. I'll hold your hands and bear you up like I have always done by taking you through powerful affirmations. These affirmations will

help you fight with strength and courage. Shall
we begin our walk through the affirmations?

1. I have all the courage I need to stand up
   to anyone that intimidates me.
2. I give no one the permission to
   intimidate me into silence.
3. I am worthy to be in leadership.
4. I cannot be trampled by anyone.
5. My leadership gives room to no
   mediocrity.
6. I attract people that believe in my
   leadership dreams.
7. I have the best support system.
8. I am not afraid to stand up to a system
   that is designed to oppress.
9. I give no one the power to silence me
   into submission.
10. I lead with wisdom.
11. I do not compromise my office for any
   reason.

12. I do not indulge in criminal acts to stay relevant in office.

13. I am not afraid to stand up for myself.

14. I attract black women in leadership whose dreams align with mine.

15. I join forces with other black women to fight oppression.

16. I am not silent in the face of oppression.

17. I'll cause a positive change in black women's leadership.

18. I dissociate myself from everything that would make leadership difficult for me.

19. I am not afraid to be my truest self even in leadership.

20. I am too powerful to be intimidated by anyone.

21. Black women leadership will grow from strength to strength in my time.

22. My leadership bears a lot of excellence.

23. I am willing to incorporate new and productive strategies into my leadership.

24. I support no form of intimidation.

25. I am aware that the bully is only as strong as I make it.
26. I lead wisely even in private establishments.
27. My good leadership skills are evident even in my personal life.
28. No intimidation can end me. I end it.

Key Points

Intimidation ends when you stand up to the bully. Remember this always and muster the courage you need to fight anyone that tries to shrink you into yourself. You have the power you need to fight. Below are the key points for this section.

- You have all it takes to fight anyone that intimidates you.
- Do not bow to intimidation. Stand your ground. The bully becomes afraid of you when you stand your ground.

- Be willing to incorporate new ideas and great strategies into your leadership.
- Do not make the mistake of indulging in crime to stay relevant in leadership. You most likely won't love the outcome.

We have come to the end of this chapter, I hope these affirmations for leadership strengthens you and empowers you for the next big thing that you wish to embark on. The next chapter will be all about self-confidence affirmations for gorgeous black women like you. Come with me, let's explore it all together!

Chapter Ten

Self-Confidence Affirmations For Black Women

Your success will be determined by your own confidence and fortitude.
—Michelle Obama

Sometimes, when I see people cry about how no one believes in them, the first question I ask is 'do you believe in yourself?' This is a truth that you must know. Your confidence in yourself is what propels other people to believe in you. A lot of people have very twisted views of self-confidence. Self-confidence is not being defensive or trying to shut people up when they try to point out things that you don't want them to point out to you.

Self-Confidence is your ability to trust in your own judgement, qualities and yourself. Self-confidence is that driving force that propels you to take up tasks that other people find challenging. Read the quote at the beginning of this chapter again. Let it sink deeply into you. Your success will be determined by the level of your self-confidence. I realized this truism a very long time ago, and that is why I am extremely daring. You never know how well you can excel in a thing until you try. Self-confidence pushes to try. Without self-confidence, you'll hold back even from doing things that you can do with effortless ease.

There comes a point in everyone's life where they would have to stand up for themselves and encourage themselves. The truth is, people may not believe in you all the time. Especially in situations that seem absurd or when you begin to dream some very big dreams. At that point in time, you may begin to think that people are not wicked or unkind because they do not believe in your biggest dreams. It would interest you to know that that's not often the case in most times. They do not believe in you simply because what you bring to the table is strange to them. They would need some evidence to hold on to before they can really believe you. So, you have to believe in yourself first. For instance, someone tells you there's a time traveler in town who can take you through time. In this case? What would be your first reaction? You'd most likely call it bluff because of the absurdity of it all. But the moment you see some solid evidence, your unbelief would be cleared. In this example, you are the time traveler who needs to perform the magic and the people are those who wouldn't believe in you until evidence is provided.

Do you understand how it works now? Your self-confidence is paramount. Being confident in one's self is not an easy thing to do. Sometimes, the doubt will creep in when you least expect it to. It is in moments like that that you would need to step up and remind yourself of what you stand for. While you do that, also remember to remind yourself of the power you possess to make that thing come true. Think of the good things that self-confidence helped you achieve and do not be afraid to take the big leap.

I know how demanding this self-confidence thing can become, and that is why I'd be supporting you along every step of the day. I'll hold your hand through this page and lead you through some energizing and motivating self-confidence affirmations written specially for you. Shall we begin?

1. I believe in my dreams. And I am aware that I have everything I need to realize them.
2. I am confident in myself even if no one else is.
3. I trust in my abilities and strengths.
4. I give no one the power to take away my self-confidence. I guide it with so much zeal and jealousy.
5. I give myself the freedom to step away from everything that makes me lose faith in myself.
6. I am highly confident in myself, and I believe in my dreams no matter how absurd other people might find them.
7. I am confident in my abilities to accomplish great things.
8. My self-confidence helps me rise to the top with so much ease.
9. I eliminate self-doubt in my life.

10. I am aware of the value of self-confidence, I work hard to gain mine and I sustain it with ease.
11. My self-confidence is a very powerful feature about me.
12. My self-confidence makes me know when to leave a place that continually shrinks me.
13. I am not afraid to undertake big projects.
14. I can do anything I put my heart to.
15. Self-doubt has no place in me.
16. I set the standard with my self-confidence.
17. I attain the greatest heights because I embrace self-confidence.
18. My self-confidence ushers me into a lot of goodness.
19. Self-confidence looks beautiful on me.
20. People believe in me greatly because of my self-confidence.

Key Points

My dearest black woman, your self-confidence is one of the greatest attires that you can wear. It stands you out from thousands. Below are the key points for this session.

- There is no single thing that you cannot do if you put your heart to it.
- Do not be afraid to take on big projects and opportunities.
- Your self-confidence is attractive, do not let anyone make you feel otherwise.
- Dare to try!

I Step Out Of My Comfort Zone

Some black women do not reach their apex because they do not step out of the confines of their comfort zones. Not stepping out of that place that offers you a lot of ease stops you from reaching great heights.

At some point in my life, I stayed put in an average job simply because I was afraid of what would happen if I began to venture out and explore big opportunities. I didn't understand the source of this fear at first. It wasn't because of qualifications. I had great ones. I was passionate about what I loved doing, but I still found it difficult to venture out. It took me sometime to realize that despite the great skills I possessed, I lacked something very important. Self-confidence. The absence of self-confidence in you can make you seem like the least bright person in the room even when you're the brightest. There is this thing that self-confidence does to a person that I am yet to find a perfect name for. It makes you stand out brilliantly. It makes your work become more glaring and beautiful. That's how beautiful it is. You know, people believe in you as much as you want them to. If you're not confident in yourself one bit, why would you expect anyone to be confident in you? It doesn't work that way at all. You have to do it first. You have to put in that work.

Sometimes, you'd relax in a mediocre place and endure poor treatments not because that is what you deserve, but because that is what you have chosen. Believe me, not daring yourself to go all out isn't beneficial at all. You might even begin to regret it later. You should know that you have all it takes to do the things that you want to do. Don't be afraid of venturing out into big things. You are deserving of it. Stepping out of your comfort zone is one of the best things that you could possibly do for yourself. It helps you grow and makes you open to more opportunities.

Don't feel overwhelmed by these at all. You don't have to do it all at once. No one does that even. You have to start with some basic steps. Then you progress into bigger ones. To step out of your comfort zone, the first step that you should take is reprogramming your mind. Do you find this strange? I'm not exactly surprised. You know, that fear or complacency that holds you back from stepping out of your comfort zone begins from your mind. That is why I put it to you that the first step is reprogramming your mind. You'd have to unlearn a lot of things. You'd have to unlearn how to accept mediocrity with open arms, how to stay in places that do not benefit you and how to follow the norms.

Stepping out of your comfort zone would make you realize that beauty is not always in conformity. Sometimes, it is in you giving yourself the power and confidence to be the odd one out. Today, I urge you to step out of your comfort zone. I understand that you need a good dose of self-confidence to step out of it. I'll help you by going through some powerful affirmations with you. Hold my hand tightly let us begin our affirmation journey. I'm ready, are you?

1. I have all it takes to excel beyond my comfort zone.
2. I am worthy of great things. I am a great person, and I won't let anyone make me feel less of it.
3. I do not embrace the complacency that comes with being in my comfort zone.
4. I dare myself to step out and reach for the greatest things.
5. I am confident in all of my abilities.

6. I do not find mediocrity attractive nor beneficial.
7. I have all I need to step out from a boring conformity.
8. I do not conform to anything that shrinks me.
9. I cease everyday to remind myself that my comfort zone is not where my apex lies.
10. I'll reach my apex and I'll flourish greatly.
11. I am not afraid to step out of my comfort zone.
12. I embrace self-confidence with the whole of my being.
13. I am grateful for the blessings that self-confidence brings.
14. I stun everyone with my gorgeous self-confidence.
15. I am beautiful the most when I'm confident in myself.

16. I wear my self-confidence with so much pride and elegance.
17. I gracefully step out of my comfort zone.
18. I am ready and willing to take up new challenges and tasks.
19. I am not overwhelmed by the stress and fear that leaving a comfort zone sometimes bring.
20. I believe in all of my dreams.
21. I give my comfort zone no power over me.
22. I am not enticed by my comfort zone. I step out into greatness.

Key Points

Dare to step out of your comfort zone. Dare to take up great opportunities. Dare to take charge of your self-confidence level. You have everything that it takes, remember this always. Below are the key points for this section.

- You have everything it takes to step out of your comfort zone.
- The apex that you seek to reach doesn't reside in your comfort zone, you have to step out and reach for it.
- You do not have to conform to be accepted, you can set the standard.
- Wear your self-confidence with a lot of pride. It looks very great on you.
- Do not embrace the mediocrity that the comfort zone offers. You are worth a lot more.

I Am Rooting For Myself Even If No One Does

Do you love the title of this section? I chose this title for the sole purpose of strengthening you, I hope you love it. Have you ever thought of this question, what becomes of me if no one roots for me even with my self-confidence? Do I throw self-confidence all away or beg people to root for me?

I am somewhat certain that questions like this one do arise in your heart from time to time. My friend, they are nothing to feel bad about. They simply show that you are a human with a very active mind. The truth is, I've been in quite similar situations to these ones. No one believed in me. They didn't see the things I saw in my own ideas. It was very frustrating, but I think it equipped me for the future. It made me make peace with the fact that people won't always support me, especially when there's nothing to show for it yet. In the earlier section, I talked about how people give their support more when they see evidence. I'm making you remember it again, it is one thing that you must know. We are not entitled to people's kindness. You know that right? Knowing this fact and making peace with it would make you not falter nor lose your self-confidence when people don't support you as you would desire them to. So, what do I do when no one roots for me no matter how confident I am? It is simple, I root for myself and not give up. I know you just rolled your eyes at me for making it sound like a stroll in the park. It isn't, I am aware.

You'd have to take some steady and gradual steps. The first step that I'd recommend you start with is strengthening your belief and confidence in yourself and your ideas. How can one do this? You can do it by first reminding yourself of that passion that drives you to try your hardest.

That passion that keeps you up at night. That self-confidence that has seen you through your most difficult rejections. Then you go ahead to ask yourself one question. 'Do I really want to do this? Can I get this?'. In these, you'll find your answer and you'll be strengthened. There's this thing that passion does to you. It makes you serious, and it fuels your creativity and strength more. It'll even help you belief more in yourself.

One more step that you should take is this. Try your best to distance yourself from the people and things that cause you not to root for yourself. You do not need any negativity to thrive. In fact, negativity will shrink you much more than you can imagine. Yes, you have to stay away from that person that ceases every moment to tell you how absurd your dreams are and how achieving them is nothing but an imagination. This might come off as selfish, but it isn't at all. Again, I remind you not to accommodate people that shrink you and make you doubt yourself when you need support the most. One thing you should know is this, people like that could diminish your self confidence level. Yes, people can do this to your self-confidence. No matter how self-confident an individual is, the moment that individual begins to absorb too much negativity, the individual would most likely end up affected.I do not want this for you, and I know that you do not want it for yourself too.

Rooting for yourself all alone with no one's support is truly not an easy thing to do, but it becomes easier when you have a great level of self-confidence. In this section, I'll help you walk through the beautiful and demanding act of rooting for one's self all alone by taking you through some powerful self-confidence affirmations written just to root for your gorgeous soul. Now, shall we begin?

1. I will forever root for myself even if no one else does.
2. I am aware that the greatest support I will ever need comes from me, I'll support myself until the end.
3. I do not open my space to anyone that shrinks me.
4. I know how to walk away from the people and the things that shrink me.
5. I am blessed to be able to root for myself.
6. I am grateful for every support I get.
7. I am confident in myself until the end.
8. I'll never throw my self-confidence away no matter what.
9. I am confident in the manifestations of my biggest dreams.

10. I root for myself with the whole of my
heart.

11. I derive joy in rooting for myself.

12. I am confident that all the work I put into
myself will not become wasted effort.

13. I love myself a lot, I'll root for myself
every day.

14. I give no one the power to discourage
me.

15. I give no one the power to make me feel
terrible for supporting myself end
believing in myself the way I do.

16. I bear no grudge against anyone for not
supporting me, I am happy that I get to
support myself.

17. I am at my highest point when I support
myself.

18. I reach my apex with ease when I
support myself.

19. I am aware that I bear all the support
that I could ever need.

20. I root for myself with a lot of joy.

21. I derive pleasure in taking responsibility for myself.
22. I possess all the strength I need to do all that I am supposed to do. I leave nothing to chance.
23. I love myself for all the goodness that I bear.

Key Points

My dear black woman, I hope this section makes it much easier and beautiful for you to support yourself as much as you need. I hope it takes you deeper into the realization that you have all it takes to root for yourself as much as you desire.

Below are the key points for this session.

- You are the support that you need.
- No one can truly root for you as much as you root for yourself.

- Do not give anyone the permission to make you feel terrible for rooting for yourself. You are worth it, you have always been, and you will always be.
- Do yourself some good by walking away from people who diminish your self-confidence level while you root for yourself.

Chapter Eleven

Courage Affirmations For The Black Woman

I learned that courage was not the absence of fear, but the triumph over it.
—Nelson Mandela

Whenever courage is mentioned, the first thing that comes to most people's minds is the absence of fear. Many people believe that a courageous person is a person without fear, but this is not true in any way. To be courageous is to do things that make you afraid. You are afraid, but you do it anyway. You don't think you can land the job, but you apply anyway. You don't think your boss would approve a raise, but you ask anyway. This, my dear, is what courage is about. Courage makes you do the things that make you afraid, it doesn't kill your fear.

Courage is one essential attribute that we need to live life. Without courage, you would keep on holding back and never go for the things you love because you are wholly dominated by fear. Fear paralyzes the biggest vision, it makes a big person feel small. Never give in to it. I understand that fear is a normal feeling. I get afraid sometimes. But I am not dominated by fear. Courage demands that I try at least. It demands that from you, too. You have to understand one thing, courage doesn't in any way make light of your fear or ridicule it. Rather, it asks you to overlook that fear and go for the next big thing. There's this thing about not trying. It fills one with so much regret. It's better to try a thing and fail at it than not try at all and regret your actions later. You'll also save yourself the big trouble of imagining what could have been. There are two ways to this thing, it's either it works or it doesn't. Focus on trying your best. It's either you win or not. When you begin to see it this way, you'll realize that fear is what you make it to be. It is only as powerful as you make it. Now, you choose, would you give fear so much power over you or not?

Life involves a lot of risks. It takes so much courage to take risks too. If you spend your life avoiding risks at all costs, you might end up not leading a very interesting life. Most of those things that you wish to own live in the risks that life would present before you from time to time. It's either you go for it, or you ignore it. The ball is in your court. Remember this every day. But, I'll advise you to take risks. Please note that not all risks are worth taking, some are out rightly stupid. Yes, there are good risks, and there are bad risks. Engaging in a game that can claim your life because you want to belong with your friends is a bad risk to take. Come to think of it, what would you gain from a bad risk like this one? Nothing at all. You'd end up losing so much. Investing in stock is a good risk. You know, it takes a great deal of courage to invest money. You'd battle with so many what if's before you eventually do it. Now, what do you stand to gain when you invest? Financial freedom. Do you see the difference between the good and the bad risk? I hope you see it very clearly. Before you take any risk, always try to think carefully about it. Think about what it could cost you, think about what you stand to gain. Doing this will help you make good decisions and courage would help you execute them.

I know all the fear and doubt that comes with walking this courage path. Sometimes, you'll feel crazy about certain things. Other times, fear would overwhelm you. In all of this, do not let courage go. Do the things that make you afraid. Leap for the heights that awe you. Apply for the positions that you dream of. You'll be amazed at the outcomes. I won't leave you alone to take this courage walk alone, I'll hold your hand like I have always done and guide you through some wonderful affirmations for courage. Hold my hand, let's begin.

1. I am courageous enough to take big steps.
2. I acknowledge my fear, but I will not let it dominate my life.
3. Courage looks so gorgeous on me.
4. I'll do all that I set my heart to.
5. I am not overwhelmed by fear.
6. I am as courageous as I can be.
7. I embrace courage with the whole of my being.
8. I excel the most when I am courageous.
9. I come from a history of black women who dominate fear. I too shall dominate my fear and win.
10. I excel through the power of courage.

11. I do not know how to give up on the things I love.

12. People love me for my courage.

13. Courage opens up great doors for me.

14. I am happy that I am courageous.

15. I take risks, and I excel in them.

16. I am not afraid of taking risks.

17. I am exceedingly great.

18. I loves and value courage greatly.

19. I am a very courageous woman.

20. I'll achieve every single thing that once scared me.

21. I am grateful for all the times I let courage triumph over fear.

22. I forgive myself for all the times I let fear dominate my life.

Key Points

My dear black woman, embrace courage with the whole of your heart. It will make you excel more than you have always dreamed. It is the courageous ones that make history.

Remember this every time you are tempted not to choose courage. Below are the key points for this section.

- Life contains a lot of risks, take the good ones.
- Do the things you want to do no matter how scared you are.
- Courage is not the absence of fear, it is doing great things even in the presence of fear.
- Forgive yourself for all the times you let fear win, celebrate yourself for all the times that you were courageous enough to go after the things you wanted.

Courage Affirmations To Overcome Fear

Fear is one of the most terrible emotions I have ever known. Fear is an innate thing, but that doesn't mean that you should let it gain so much dominance in your life. If you do, you would regret it for quite a very long time. Most times, great fear doesn't just come to you all by itself. Something triggers it. It could be a thought, a past experience, an individual. The trigger is like an open door through which the fear can come in. I like to think of it as an open wound and fear as an infection. When the wound is open, it would be very easy for the infection to get in. Do you get the drift?

Whenever I notice fear coming into me, I try to block it off by not paying mind to the thing that triggers the fear. It is a method that has worked a lot of times for me. I think you should try it too. I know you wonder about the possibility of shutting fear away forever. I've wondered about it too, and in my wondering I found answers. It's not possible to completely shut fear away from one's mind. Do you know why this is so? It is so because fear is an innate thing. It's just inside us like every other emotion. We all knew fear even as little children. But the good thing here is that we can manage fear and live a great life with it. If we can live with other emotions that we feel, why can't we live with fear, too? No reason at all.

The first step that you should take towards managing fear is the identification of your triggers. You have to find out those things that make you afraid. Fear management is easier, faster and more efficient when you know the things that trigger your fear. You know, it is always easier to treat a known disease than an unknown one. But, fear doesn't always come with triggers. Sometimes, it just saunters through your mind and starts looking for something to feed on in order to make you afraid. Fear would spin up a thing that would never happen and watch you quiver in terror. After identifying what triggers your fear, the next step you should take is control the triggers. You can do this by thinking less about those triggers and distancing yourself from them. This is a very effective method. Walk away from the trigger and watch every other thing cower.

Courage is yet another great thing that you should wholly embrace if you must control your fear. You know, fear works to ensure that you do not take the big steps that you need to take while courage works to ensure that you take those steps. Out of these two contrasting things, fear is the easiest to go to. And that's why a lot of people tilt towards it. Courage is the harder and best option. Not only does it help you in the pursuit of your goals, it also helps you control your fear effectively. That is why I advise you, my dear black woman, to follow courage with all your heart.

There is one more thing that I would love you to know. Fear has a very faux power. Yes, it is not all that powerful. Fear is only as powerful as you make it. Fear swallows you up when you give it power. I'll share my story with you. Have you ever witnessed a high jump? It is a sport where people are made to jump over set heights. I used to be sorely afraid of jumping even the lowest heights because of how fearful I was. Whenever I deigned to try, I'd think about the high chances of me jumping wrongly and ending up with a permanent scar that would make me hate high jumps until the end of my life. This fear continued for a long time until the day I decided to try. I still do not know what inspired me to jump on that day. The crazy thing is, I tried jumping very very high. I did it! I couldn't believe my eyes at all. It felt like a sweet dream. After that day, I began to jump more and partake in more sports. Especially the ones that scared me. That experience taught me a beautiful lesson that I am sharing now with you. Fear is only as big as you make it. Do the things that scare you and make you gasp in surprise. Life would be a lot of boredom but for things like this. Do not allow fear to dominate your life. Be courageous in this life! You have all it takes! I know it.

Taking the courage path is not an easy thing to do at all. I say this from my own experiences. But you don't have to worry about how to walk this courage path all alone because I'd be holding you up as I have always done through the pages of this book. Together, we'll be courageous.

1. I cease to give fear power over my life.
2. I am aware that fear is only as powerful as I make it. So, I'll take away every power from fear and be in charge of my life.
3. I embrace courage with the whole of my being.
4. I quit giving up on the things I love without even trying.
5. I make peace with either winning or losing. I'll no longer be afraid to try.
6. I stun the most when I am my most courageous self.
7. I am so courageous that fear trembles at the sight of me.
8. I eliminate fear from every area of my life.
9. Courage comes easy to me.
10. I conquer fear with a lot of ease.
11. Fear doesn't control me, I control fear.
12. I am too big to be controlled by fear.

13. I'll go for the things I want even in the midst of fear.

14. I am grateful for all the times I dared to try even in fear.

15. I am not consumed by fear.

16. I am exceedingly courageous.

17. I am blessed to know courage.

18. I love courage, I'll be courageous until the end.

19. Trying doesn't scare me anymore.

20. I bloom greatly even in my fear.

21. My fears do not define me, they are just a small part of the wonderful woman that I am.

Key Points

My dear black woman, I hope fear doesn't dominate your life anymore. I trust in your unique abilities to kill fear. Below are the key points for this section.

- Fear is only as great as you make it.

- Your fear doesn't define you.

- Afraid? Try anyway.

- You are in control of your fear. Remember this always.

- Don't hold back anymore because of fear, dare to try. You'll be happy you did.

Courage Affirmations For Love

Has it ever occurred to you that you need a very generous amount of courage to love? But, that's not the way the movies show it. I know, I know. In the movies, you meet someone you love, emotions rage and you both fall in love. Life would have been less complicated if loving was this easy. There wouldn't be a lot of pain and heartaches. A lot of black women are emotionally damaged today because they loved the wrong people. Yes, it is possible to love the wrong person. Who exactly is the wrong person? A wrong person is that person that makes love into a bizarre thing for you. The wrong person leaves you with bruises and makes you regret ever knowing what love is. You'd wonder, are these wrong people the bad people of this world? No, they're not. The truth is, the wrong person for me might be the ideal person for you. The perfect person even. This is where compatibility comes in. Being with a person you're not compatible with makes love sour. If you and your partner are not compatible with each other, you'd end up being the wrong people for each other. This is how it works. Do you get the concept of the wrong person, now?

A lot of times in the past, I shut away people I loved and people who loved me because I lacked the courage to love them. I'd second guess every single act of kindness toward me and think everyone was set out to hurt me. Sometimes, this fear of getting hurt or broken stems from past experiences with love. We don't know how deep a failed love relationship hits us until it is time to open our hearts to love again. But it doesn't always arise from bad experiences. Some people are just naturally afraid of becoming vulnerable and free in love. I am that kind of person. I know how it feels. I'd make lots of excuses to avoid meeting with people I even admired because I was afraid of loving them deeply. I didn't do these things because I hated love. I did them because I lacked courage. I lacked that courage that one needs to love wholeheartedly. I'd read love stories and smile when people fall in love. I loved the idea of love and I loved to see people fall in love. I only loved love when I wasn't the one in it.

As I grew older, I knew I had to do something about it. I had to work on my love life. I started by coming to terms with the fact that not all relationships would lead into a big thing or end beautifully. Then, I made one big decision. I decided to let myself love as much as I wanted to. I decided to stop holding back. My dear woman, it was so difficult for me. I didn't just know how to go about it. All I knew was that I wanted love without wanting it. This is confusing, right? I faced a lot of confusion. It took me quite a long time to understand that not everyone that wants a thing with me comes with the intention of hurting me or breaking my heart into a thousand shards. It was at that point in my life that I first became aware of how lovable a person I was. I am grateful for all the steps I took towards loving. But I am most grateful for the courage I mustered to love. If you keep on stopping yourself from loving because of fear, you might regret it for a very long time. Give yourself the freedom and the courage to cherish the little moments and dwell in them. Fall in love and appreciate that love. If it lasts forever, beautiful. But if it doesn't, also beautiful. Pick the lessons and move on with your life. Appreciate yourself for daring to love in a world like ours that's too weak and cowardly to love. Would you?

Being courageous in love is not an easy thing at all. But I can make it easy for you by taking you through powerful affirmations that would help you build all the courage that you need to love. Hold my hand and let us begin, shall we?

1. I'll dare to love as deeply and passionately as I desire.
2. I embrace all the beauty and goodness that is found in love, I will quit shutting myself away from love.
3. I am aware of how much of a lovable person that I am. I will accept love with the whole of my being.
4. Fear no longer dominates my love life.
5. I have all the courage I need to love as much as I desire.
6. I am patient with myself as I build courage in love.
7. My love life is filled with courage and not fear.
8. I love love, I won't let fear take it away from me.

9. I refuse to believe that everyone is set
    out to hurt me and make me regret
    loving.
10. I am positive that I will get the kind of
    love that I have always dreamed about.
11. I am courageous enough to stop walking
    away from love.
12. Love is the best thing that has ever
    happened to me.
13. Never again will I be a coward in love.
14. I forgive myself for all the love I have
    ruined and the hearts I have broken by
    not being courageous enough to love.
15. Love doesn't frighten me anymore, it
    empowers me.
16. I am blessed to love and be loved back
    in return.
17. All the energy I put into loving is not
    wasted energy.
18. I am courageous enough to open my
    heart to love.
19. I am not afraid of vulnerability.

20. I am courageous enough to live and cherish every moment that love brings to me.

Key Points

My dear black woman, you are deserving and worthy of love. It is high time you summoned courage and opened your heart to love. It is one of the most beautiful things ever. Below are the key points for this section.

- Love is a very beautiful thing, do not be afraid to open your heart to it.
- Love comes with a certain level of vulnerability, embrace it.
- Not all love stories will end with a happy ending.
- Forgive yourself for the mistakes that you have made in love.
- Do not let fear rob you of the love that you desire.

We have come to the end of the courage chapter! I hope you enjoyed reading it as much as I enjoyed writing it. Now, go ahead and apply what you've learnt in this chapter. Be as courageous as you can be, you'll thrive more in this world with loads of courage. The next chapter will be all about stress management. Come with me, let's explore!

Chapter Twelve

Stress Management Affirmations For The Black Woman

Our greatest weapon against stress is our ability to choose one thought over another.
—William James

A lot of black women learn how to work very hard, but they do not learn stress management. Stress management is a necessary skill that everyone should possess. Studies show that people deal with more stress when they do a job that they do not really love. Does this mean that people that do the jobs they love do not face any form of stress? They definitely do. Stress is almost inevitable in every kind of work. Mind you, when I talk about stress, I do not talk about physical stress alone. Mental stress and other forms of stress are included. In fact, it is easier to deal with physical stress than mental stress. A good massage session, food and enough sleep could be all you need to effectively deal with physical stress sometimes. But it isn't so with mental stress. In some cases, you would have to see a therapist.

Inasmuch as hard work is important, stress management should also be encouraged. Stress decreases productivity a great deal. This is one thing that many people fail to realize. They think that the time taken to rest is wasted time. No, it isn't at all. I see my resting time as an investment in my well being for increased productivity. Resting when I become stressed is one of the best things I've ever learnt. Not only does it calm me down, it also keeps me away from breakdowns. You have to

make conscious efforts to manage your stress
levels because when you look at things from
surface level, you'd think you really do not
have time to rest. You never know how much
unnecessary work you put so much effort into
until you take your time to do a personal stress
evaluation.

One great method that can help you manage
your stress is making a list of important things
that you should do. It's a simple and interesting
way to manage stress. Make a list of the most
important things that you need to attend to.
Doing this will make it easy for you to cross out
the things that are not really important.
Everyday, we wake up and think of things that
we need to do without giving proper thought to
those things. Before you indulge in some
things, ask yourself questions. Is this
important? How would this help me reach
today's target? You'll realize that questioning
yourself like this would help you develop the

habit of focusing majorly on the most important things in the long run.

You should also try to make peace with the fact that you can't do everything at once, you're no superhuman. No, I am not asking you not to aim as high as you want. I'm simply asking you to take deep breaths and rest when it gets overwhelming. Stress shortens your lifespan, take those rests and continue later. Believe me, your body will thank you for it. Allow yourself to do the things within your power first. You do not have anything to prove to anyone about your strength. Black women do not show off their strength, it shows by itself. You don't have to juggle so many things at once to appear strong. Doing that doesn't show your strength, rather, it shows how desperate you are to show off your strength. That, my friend, is a great sign of weakness. The only opinion about your strength that should count is yours. Know this and know peace. I beg you, my dear black woman, take rests and manage your stress well. You'd love the glow that it will bring to you.

I know how difficult it is to manage stress effectively all alone. That's why I'll support you by going through some powerful and effective stress management affirmations with you. Let's dig in!

1. I take rests when it becomes overwhelming. I'll not let stress ruin me.
2. I embrace the goodness and importance of effective stress management.
3. I do not glow in stress, so I'll take rests instead.
4. I love to manage my stress levels just as I love to work hard.
5. Everyday, I remind myself that stressing so much doesn't translate to great work. I do great work and stress less.

6. I cannot surrender to stress.

7. I love to manage my stress.

8. Taking rests doesn't make me weak.

9. I refuse to see rest time as wasted time, it is an investment into my well-being.

10. I care so much about my health, I'll not let stress make a mess of my mental health.

11. I do not find stress attractive in any form.

12. I walk away elegantly from the things that stress me for no just cause.

13. I distance myself from all forms of stress.

14. I can do my work greatly without a lot of stress.

15. I have wonderful stress management skills.

16. I am at peace with the fact that I can't possibly do everything all at once. So, I refuse to bother myself with the things I have no control over.

17. I dissociate myself from the people and things that increase my stress levels.

18. I do not find it difficult to say no to stress.

19. I am happier when I am not stressed.

20. I am happy that I can take a rest when I want to.

21. I am not overwhelmed by stress.

Key Points

Stress doesn't make your life beautiful in any way, master the act of doing away with it. Below are the key points for this section.

- Prioritize everything that you do, do not leave out space for stress.
- You are no super human, take rests when you need to.
- Learn how to walk away from the things that stress you out.
- Say no to stress when you can.

I Am Not Controlled By Stress

A lot of black women live their lives under the total control of stress. They give stress a lot of power that it becomes a master in their lives. Do you find it surprising? I don't at all. I've seen women who say that stress keeps them going. These women embrace the toxicity in stress so much that it begins to appear beautiful to them. It is quite similar to the Stockholm syndrome. But I don't think this is all there is to it. I mean, who thrives on just stress? The truth is, some of us use stress as an escape route from our realities. I'll use myself as an example. I'll share a life experience with you in the next paragraph.

I work very hard when I'm stressed or dealing with a problem that I do not want to face. Do you know why I do that? I simply use work as a daily distraction instead of facing the major thing eating me up from the inside. Working hard in such conditions is one coping mechanism. But coping mechanisms can become toxic too, can't they? Some of our coping mechanisms are not all that safe. In our bid to escape one problem, we end up creating another one for ourselves. This is one of the saddest things ever. And in the end, we end up with more stress. What a bad way to deal with a problem. If you're like me who uses stress as an escape route from reality, you've got to stop. The dangers that it brings outweighs the good that it does. Facing the problem is not an easy thing to do, but it is the best thing to do. Whenever the desire to escape the problem with stress comes up, tell yourself that you have to woman up and face it! Escaping from the problem doesn't make it go away. Rather, it makes it lurk in the corners. And one day, it'll pounce on you with greater ferocity. This is the thing with escaping from our problems and hiding from them. We only empower the problem. Don't be afraid to stand up to your problems.

A lot of people have glamorized stress so much that people would engage themselves in avoidable stress in order to hold the busy narrative. Everyone wants to be busy. You need to understand that being busy every time doesn't translate to being a great worker. You can work smartly without having to stress yourself so much. Don't give stress any control over your life. This is your one precious life, why would you give stress so much control over it? Take charge of your life. You have to unlearn these fallacies that people have made about stress. Begin by telling yourself about the importance of rest in your life. Restructure your life to accommodate rest. Plenty of it. You'll be more productive when you rest. My dear black woman, you do not have to be busy all the time. Yes, you do not have to work around the clock every time. It is okay not to be busy on some days. It is okay not to be overly engrossed in activities every minute of your life. A lazy day with good food and sweet sleep is no curse. You deserve some of that peaceful and great self-care. No one can get it for you but you.

At some point in your life, you would have to make certain decisions concerning stress. You'll have to stand up for yourself and say no to stress. You know one thing? It is what you allow that thrives. It is the stress that you allow that chokes you. Believe me, you are capable of ending stress in your life if you want to. Remember I once mentioned that you are much more powerful than you know? It is a truth that you should embrace. It is high time you stopped giving power to stress in all its forms.

So, my dear black woman, cease to let stress control your life. I know it is not an easy thing to do. But, I can make it easier for you. I'll give you all of my support by going through powerful affirmations that can help you stop letting stress take control of your life . You'll love them! Now, let's dig in.

1. I am in control of my life, I'll no longer give stress any power over me.
2. I do not give stress the power to rob me of my happy rest.
3. I take breaks when I'm overwhelmed.
4. I do not give stress the permission to dominate me.
5. I am not busy every day. I set time aside for rest.
6. I refuse to go with the misconception that stressful work is hard work. I don't do stressful work, I do smart work.
7. I trust in my ability to eliminate stress from my life.

8. I do not give my energy and time to the things that do not matter.

9. I am not consumed by stress.

10. I have total dominance over stress.

11. I unlearn all the lies that I believe about stress.

12. I possess great power, I am stronger than stress.

13. I do not work round the clock everyday.

14. I love resting.

15. I do not use stress as an escape route from realities, I stand up to my problems, and I face them with great solutions.

16. I do not fancy stress no matter how attractive it might seem to be.

17. I take rest seriously.

18. I am productive the most when I'm well rested.

19. I create time to rest and have fun.

20. Stress has no power to stifle out my inner joy. I am in control.

Key Points

Your life will become more beautiful and interesting the moment you decide to take control of it. Stress is only as powerful as you make it. Remember this all the time. Below are the key points for this section.

- You have all it takes to control your stress.
- You do not have to be busy every day. It is okay to have nothing to do on some days.

Create Something Beautiful Out Of My Stress.

I've been going on and on about the negative impact of stress in the past sections of this chapter. But, has it ever occurred to you that there could be positivity in stress? No, don't get me wrong. I'm not asking you to embrace stress. I'll explain what I mean to you.

Our perception of a thing and how we react to it plays a great role on how that thing affects our life. Simply, the way you react to a thing is a major determinant of how that thing affects you. I'll use stress as the major case study here. When we think of stress, we think of a thing that is set out to frustrate us and make us joyless. We try our best to run away from all forms of avoidable stress. But you'd agree with me that not all forms of stress can be really avoided, right? This brings us to an interesting question, what then can be done to free oneself from the grip of stress that can not be avoided?

It is a quite simple yet difficult answer. Detach yourself from the negativity of the stress. You know, instead of lamenting and suffering about your stress, let it motivate you to work harder. Some stress will only exist at certain points of our lives. The moment we cross over to new levels, they will end. Instead of letting a stress like that squeeze out all the joy in our lives, why shouldn't we let it motivate us instead? Of course, finding motivation in stress is not easy at all. But I have learnt that suffering sometimes propels us to work faster and harder so we can get a better life in a shorter time.

I understand how difficult it is to find motivation in stress, so I'll make it easier for you by leading you through some powerful affirmations curated just for you. Let's dig in, shall we?

1. I refuse to allow stress to make me suffer.
2. My stress propels me to work harder and faster.
3. This stress is a phase, it will pass away very quickly.
4. I have a very beautiful and interesting life.
5. Stress has no power to steal my happy life.
6. I am motivated by my stress to work harder.
7. I will not allow stress to make me into a toxic and sad person.
8. I do not wallow in stress.
9. This stress is preparing me for something great and beautiful.
10. I am not overwhelmed by this stress, I am in control of it all.

11. I excel greatly despite the stress.

Key Points

When you begin to see your stress as a tool that propels you for something greater, you'll work harder and smarter and reach your goals faster. Below are the key points that you should note.

- You have great power and control over your stress.
- You'll excel greatly despite all the stress that you face.
- Your life becomes more joyful when you allow stress to motivate you into working harder.

Again, we have come to the end of a chapter! I am excited. I enjoyed going through these stress management affirmations with you so much. Did you enjoy it like I did? I bet that the next chapter will be even more thrilling. But before we move to it, I'd admonish you to embrace stress management in its best forms. Not only does it make you exude a brighter and more beautiful black excellence, it also makes you healthier and happier. Now, let's go tothe next chapter. It'll be all about affirmations for positive thinking. Let's dig in already!

Chapter Thirteen

Affirmations For Positive Thinking For The Black Woman

You can't win in life if you're losing in your mind. Change your thoughts and it'll change your life.
—Tony Gaskins

We do not talk enough about the power of positive thinking. Thinking positively is one of the greatest things you can embrace if you are keen on changing your life for the better. Somehow, our thoughts reflect in our outward life. If there's anything that you must know, it is the fact that your thoughts play a very crucial role in how your life turns out . Go back to the quote at the beginning of this chapter and read it all over again. Do you feel the impact in those words? They aren't just words, they bear the truth that you need to know.

Many times, life will give you reasons to think as negatively as possible. Some things that happen will make you feel like the most miserable person in the world. But tell me, my dear black woman, will you let circumstances steal the power and goodness of positive thinking from you? Of course not. Dwell in positive thoughts and watch your life turn around for the best. Sometimes, you will feel so overwhelmed that you will want to 'feel' your grief and spend more time picking at the wounds. It is perfectly okay to feel this way. You're a human with complex emotions and thought processes. I don't judge you for letting yourself feel. Sometimes, letting yourself feel those strong emotions will help you heal from them faster. So, let yourself feel.

There are times I felt very stupid for thinking as positively as I did. I'd laugh at myself and wondered where I get all the energy from. Believe me, it is not easy to choose to think positively at all times. It is not easy to choose optimism over pessimism at every single point of your life. In fact, it is one of the most difficult things ever. Positive thinking doesn't mean that you will lose touch with reality, rather, you choose to see the good things and think the best thoughts. It'll make you have a better life. That's why I'd advise you to choose to think positively every day of your life.

I know how difficult it is to choose to think positively at all times. It is very demanding and exhausting. But it becomes easier with time and consistency. You should understand that it's okay to slip back once in a while. But, the best thing is forging ahead and not gloating nor beating yourself up for the times you fell and had to try again. I have curated a fine list of affirmations for positive thinking just for you. Let's dig in!

1. I live the best days of my life.
2. My life is an overflowing river of joy, love and all the goodness that I desire.
3. Nothing can steal my joy and peace.
4. All the hard work I do will pay off, I do not labor in vain.
5. I eliminate negative thoughts from my heart.
6. I am stronger than all the negativity in the world.
7. I am aware of the power of my mind, I utilize it to the best of my ability.
8. I am a very intelligent and amazing woman.
9. I'll sing my best songs with the most sonorous of voices.
10. I am blessed and happy to be me.
11. I excel greatly in all areas of my life.
12. I'll get my dream jobs with ease.

13. I do not struggle to stand out anywhere. I stand out by being my true self.

14. I am made for excellence.

15. Nothing can shrink me or make me feel small.

16. I am proud of myself and I am thankful for every progress I make.

17. I look gorgeous in every dress I wear. I am elegance in all its forms!

18. How joyful I am that I get to be me!

19. My smile warms the hardest hearts.

20. I do my jobs with a lot of excellence!

21. I'll realize all my dreams!

22. I am evidence that black is perfect and glorious.

23. I am not shaken up by circumstances, I am in total control!

24. I am a lovable and amazing person.

25. I thrive in all areas of my life.

26. I am greatly loved and cherished.

27. I am surrounded by amazing people who love to help me and see me flourish.

28. I make and keep friends easily.

29. I am perfect.

Key Points

Positive thinking will fill your life with all the beauty that you never knew existed. The time has come for you to ditch all the negative thoughts that lay in your heart. Embrace positive thinking today! Find the key points for this section below.

- Thinking positively will turn your life around for the best.
- You cannot do greatly if there's so much negativity in you.
- Embrace everyday with love, everyday is the best day of your life.

I Work In Line With My Positive Thinking

It is one thing to think positively, and it is another thing entirely to execute positive things. You know, thinking is another, and saying is another. Now that you have embraced the whole armor of positive thinking, you should ask yourself these questions. Are my actions in line with my positive thought process? Do I work towards this positivity that I desire and think about every moment? If your answer to these questions are no, you have a lot of work to do on yourself. I trust you to do it beautifully and excellently.

A student has a major examination to write. A very tough one. A lot of people have written the exams and failed. Only a few people pass that particular exam on their first sitting. This student is filled with a lot of positivity about the exam. This student believes that she will write the exam and come out with flying colors. Amidst all of the positivity and good thinking, this student doesn't study for this exam as she should. In summary, this student is a lazy but very positive student. Failure is almost inevitable for this student no matter how positive she is in her thinking. Yes, thinking positively isn't all there is to achieving success. You have to put in the work too. Do you understand this? Your positive thought process will be more prominent in your good grades when you work hard. Never make the mistake of abandoning the work you need to put in simply because you think great thoughts. You need to know that positive thinking is not a magic of some sort. It doesn't replace the work that you need to put in. Never forget this.

One thing that you must know is this. No matter how high the level of your positive thinking is, it won't singlehandedly take you to the heights that you desire to reach independently. A couple of great habits would be required to work hand in hand with your positive thinking. While you think positively about getting that dream job, do not forget to get the necessary skills for it. While you think positively about getting the best grades, do your part by studying as hard as you should. While you think positively about dominating your field, do the needed work. You don't stay relevant in a competitive world like ours by just thinking positively. If you try to do that, you'll get lost in the times. Keep this at the back of your mind and pull it out to have a look from time to time so you can know the major things that you should focus on.

I have heard a lot of black women complain about the persistence of their negative thinking despite how hard they work and how well they do things. My friend, I have been in situations like this too. I'd literally work my ass off and still wallow in self-rejection and very negative thoughts despite it all. It made me detest myself for a while. I mean, how could one be home to such a level of negativity? At first, I thought it was all a part of who I was. You know, just one of those people that always saw negativity in everything no matter how good those things were. This is one of the terrible things about negative thinking. It shuts you away from seeing all the good and beautiful things and appreciating them for that goodness. It only opens your eyes to see negativity and shortcomings. It took me some time to understand that all that negativity wasn't who I was. I think we are all born with clean, beautiful and neutral minds. But as we grow older, we begin to pick up habits and thought processes from the things we encounter. Some people are lucky enough to pick more good habits than bad ones, others are not that lucky. I know you're looking at me in disbelief now. You really want to ask if I'm aware that people can be born with different abilities and personalities. Right? My dear black woman, I know this fully well. I need you to understand that our habits and behaviors are greatly shaped by our environment and exposure. That's why people are able to build their own habits.

My dear black woman, I need you to understand that becoming a positive thinker is a process. A very gradual process if you were once deeply rooted in negativity and its cousins. You have to learn how to be patient with yourself. It is a process that you cannot skip. Rome wasn't built in a day is no cliché. It is a lot of truth. You can't become a positive thinker overnight. Take your time and go through the process. I love to take every process of my life seriously because I know they won't be there forever. They become memories quickly. So, go through them with all elegance when they come. You'll be happy you did in the coming times.

I know how difficult it is to embrace the power of positive thinking wholly. But, I'll make this great embrace much easier for you by holding your hand tightly like I have always done and take you through some wonderful affirmations that will help you work in line with all of your positive thinking.

1. My actions are in line with my positive thinking.
2. I am positive all round. I leave no room for negativity to leak through.
3. I do not do things that are contradictory to all the positivity that I confess in my heart.
4. I understand that becoming a positive thinker is a process, I'll treat myself with care as I go through the process.
5. I think positive thoughts everyday.
6. I get great results that reflect the beauty and power of my positive thinking.

7. I have a very beautiful and powerful thought process.

8. I am aware that whatever settles in my mind has the power to influence me greatly. I am very careful of what I let into my heart.

9. I have an active and brilliant brain that dwells in positive thinking.

10. I think positively without losing touch of reality.

11. I am happy that I can see positivity in most things.

12. I am blessed to be able to think the way I do.

13. My brain is the most gorgeous brain there is.

14. I do not dwell on the things that can go wrong, I dwell on the things that would work according to my plans.

15. I am glad that I think positive thoughts alone.

Key Points

My dear black woman, remember to always work in line with your positive thoughts. You can do it, and I know you will. Below are the key points that you should note for this section.

- Your brain is your powerhouse, fill it with a lot of good thoughts.
- Your thinking is capable of affecting your life, think positive thoughts.
- Becoming a positive thinker takes time, be patient with yourself.
- Think positively and put in the work! They go hand in hand.
- Your thought process is wonderful, remind yourself all the time.

My dear black woman, we have come to the end of this chapter! I had a lot of fun while going through these affirmations for positive thinking with you. They strengthened me in the most beautiful ways. I trust that you enjoyed it as much as I did. Tell me, did you? I urge you to take your time and grow into the positive thinker that you have always dreamt of becoming. I can't wait to see you excel at it. The time has come for us to step into a new chapter. The very last chapter in this book. Affirmations For The Black Woman On Authenticity. Do you know why I wrote this chapter last? I wrote it last in a bid to remind you to never forget to be your most authentic self in everything that you do. Now, let's begin to explore the last chapter! It will be a lot of fun, I promise you.

Chapter Fourteen

Affirmations For The Black Woman On Authenticity

Authenticity is the daily practice of letting go of who we think we are supposed to be and embracing who we are.
—Brene Brown.

Authenticity is one of the best things you can wear. I love this quote by Brene Brown with my heart. Nothing sums up authenticity as concisely as this. Everyday, we rise to fight our places in the world. We meet people, experience cultures, unlearn and relearn. While doing all of these, we might begin to lose our true selves. Staying genuine and original is beyond posting beautiful and Afrocentric pictures of yourself and captioning them #natural. It is way deeper than that. Aren't you curious as to what makes people lose themselves? I'll share some of them with you in this chapter.

The greatest reason why people forfeit their authentic selves is acceptance. It is human nature to crave for love and acceptance in every place. In some places that we will go to, the people there will not accept us because we do not fit into their leagues. My friend, this is where a lot of people lose it. They'll begin to think that there's something wrong with them or their ideals. In order to get people to accept them, they will begin to drop those things that make them themselves. It works out most of the time. They'll be accepted. But come to think of it. Is an acceptance that takes away your authenticity a true one? Is it not a glamorized form of bondage?

A lot of black women lose their authenticity for conformity's sake. This is one thing I understand very well. With the great level of discrimination against black women in some parts of the world, black women are made to face a lot of pressure. Some of them never bow to this pressure. Others can't withstand it. So, they bow to it and give up the biggest parts of their identity. This is one sad thing. It is okay to lose other things in this world, but losing one's authenticity is not okay at all.

Lest I forget, there is also the class of black women who give up their authenticity because they feel it is not in vogue. You know, they give up their history and roots to take up a new one that they don't even understand well. This class of black women do not understand the gravity of giving up one's authenticity. They care about the rave of the moment and ignore their roots. Don't be this kind of black woman. Be the black woman that encourages her sisters to become themselves again.

The acceptance that comes with throwing your authenticity away doesn't last for a very long time, believe me. I don't think anyone really loves a person that gives up who she truly is because of acceptance from a certain group of people. The acceptance would last for a while, then it would fizzle out like a mirage. By then, the black woman will find it difficult to go back to her roots and she'll feel too awkward to even attempt blending into the new identity she got for herself. It is at this point that she'd begin to float on both sides. Neither authentic nor entirely fake. The confusion that comes with being in this condition can never be described properly. I do not want you to experience it at all. It's not a nice thing to know. But if you must know what it feels like, find women who have experienced it, ask your questions, and listen to all their stories.

My dear black woman, you have to learn how to stand up for yourself with all your might whenever anyone tries to make you lose your authenticity by imposing what you are not on you. Do you now know that you come from a generation of women who wrestled with vigor? You have every single thing it takes to retain your authenticity in a world that wants you to lose it. Do not give up your authenticity for any reason. Every day, the world will bring you things that it thinks you should be. Whenever it does that, bring out all that you are and embrace them with all the love your mother gave to you.

I won't leave you to walk on this authenticity path all by yourself. I'll support you as always by holding your hand and leading you through affirmations that strengthen. Now, hold my hand and walk this path with me. Would you?

1. I embrace my authenticity with so much pride and love.
2. I am proud to be who I am. I am happy to be who I am. I don't wish to be anybody else.
3. I flourish in the best ways when I am myself.
4. I wear my skin with a lot of pride.
5. I am a thing of beauty, and I am a joy forever.
6. I give no one the permission to stop me from being who I am.
7. I am grateful that I am myself.
8. I am in love with my roots and everything that came together to ensure that I exist in this time and season.
9. People marvel at the beauty and authenticity that I ooze.
10. I do not care about the acceptance that comes from anyone but myself.
11. I'll be my truest self in every day of my life.

12. I am the best version of myself.

13. I am in absolute love with myself and all that I am.

14. No matter how far I go from home, I'll never forget my roots.

15. I come from a descendant of gorgeous warriors, I'll win this fight that threatens to defeat my authenticity.

16. No matter the pressure I face, I will never give up on who I am.

17. I embrace myself with joy and pride.

18. I delight in how lucky I am that I got to be myself.

19. I know how to walk away from anything that tries to take my identity away from me.

20. I am not afraid to let go of anyone that doesn't value my originality.

21. My authenticity doesn't bloom in toxic places, I step out of all forms of toxicity no matter how glamorous they are made to look.

22. I am perfect just the way I am.

23. I am not ashamed to be myself.

24. I am not sorry for all the extras that I am. They make me who I am.

25. I'll always be myself no matter what happens.

26. I'll never allow anyone to make me into what I am not.

27. I love how I carry myself with so much pride and confidence.

Key Points

Everyday, lots of people will try to make you see reasons why you should give up on being your truest self. Do not give in to it. Nothing is worth your authenticity. Remind yourself of this as much as you can. Below are the key points for this session.

- Nothing in this world is worth your authenticity. Never give it up.
- You are gorgeous just the way you are.

- Do not conform to anything that steals your trueness.
- Wear your skin and carry yourself with a lot of pride.
- No matter how far you travel from home, do not forget the paths that lead home. That is where you'd find your authenticity the most.

Affirmations For The Black Woman Who Has Become A Stranger To Herself

A lot of black women have become strangers to themselves because they embraced the world's definition of authenticity. Remember what I said earlier, nothing is worth your authenticity. Never give it up. But all hope is not lost for every black woman who has become a person she no longer recognizes.

It's crazy how it all begins. It could be you compromising a few values because you want to conform to people's standards. You don't want to be left behind, so you do what you have to do. It begins little by little. You won't realize when you begin to become a person you had always wished not to become. In this life, there are a few things that you should never compromise no matter what. Authenticity tops the list. Whenever anyone tries to convince you why you should do that little thing, let the person know it isn't little. You just can't do it. Sometimes, that thing you consider little would be the catalyst that would cause you to do more things that you wouldn't do. Losing one's self is one of the easiest things ever. You'll always find things that will tempt you and make you want to give up on your authenticity. It takes a lot of courage and self-

will not to give in to some of these things.
Some of them know just how to make one
weak. But I know that you are more than strong
to overcome them all.

When you realize that you have become a
stranger to yourself, what do you do? Do you
gloat, or do you make efforts to become your
best self again. The latter is the best thing to
do, but it is not the easiest. Only a few women
would not gloat on making such a discovery. It
is okay for you to feel terrible and beat yourself
for doing what you did. It is okay to allow
yourself to feel those painful emotions as
strongly as you want. But I beg you not to be
unkind to yourself. Being unkind to yourself in
such a situation is not in your best interest. You
will only end up causing yourself more pain. I
am certain that that isn't what you want. Give
yourself some time and cry and feel your pain
the way you want to. Then go on to
acknowledge your mistakes. You'll find it easier

to forgive yourself and rise again when you
acknowledge your mistakes. It will take time,
but you will become your authentic self again.
You wil look into a mirror again, and you will
find yourself and not a stranger.

I know how difficult it is to become friends with
yourself all over again. But I won't leave you to
do it all alone. As always, I'll hold your hand
and lead you through affirmations that will
strengthen you. I believe in you, you'll become
your most authentic self again. Now, let us
begin.

1. I fall in love with who I am all over again.
2. I am proud to be myself.
3. Never again will I give my authenticity
   for anything.
4. I am the most beautiful when I am
   original.
5. I will never quit being myself for any
   reason.

6. I forgive myself for becoming a stranger to myself.
7. I'll look into the mirror and find myself again.
8. I refuse to let my mistakes define me.
9. I'll never compromise my standards for any reason.
10. I will not become who I am not not in quest for acceptance.
11. I am kind to myself in everything.
12. I acknowledge my mistakes, and I am willing to correct them.
13. I'll be happy with who I am again.
14. I'll never forget the road that leads home again.
15. I am a descendant of strong and independent female warriors, never again will I cower at the sight of anything that would rob me of my originality.

Key Points

My dear black woman, be kind to yourself despite the mistakes you made. I hope you find it easy to keep on being your true self in all circumstances. Below are the key points for this section.

- Be kind to yourself.
- You'll become yourself again.
- Do not compromise your originality standards for anyone.

Conclusion

Action is the foundational key to all success.
—Pablo Picasso

Yay! We have finally come to the end of this affirmation book. It was one hell of a journey. I put so much love and strength and kindness into writing this book. For each word I wrote, I hoped that you would feel it deep in your bones. I reserved this quote by Pablo Picasso because no one could have said it better than this. I wrote this book for every black woman that she may be empowered, strengthened and feel safe in her own skin. I wrote this book to light you up, my dear black woman. But, lighting you up goes beyond you reading the pages of this book. You have to take action. Before I talk more about taking action, I would love to know if you enjoyed reading this book. Did you love the ideas each chapter bore? I hope you did. I started the book with affirmations for your morning. Morning is a very important part of the day. It determines how a lot of things will turn out for you during the day. I hope that saying those morning affirmations with firm belief and energy will cause you to have better mornings and greater days. I wrote on the empowerment of the black woman because I am very conversant with the poor level of black women empowerment in our world today. My dear black woman, I hope that part of this book helps you rise and get started in your empowerment journey. It takes empowered women to change the world for the better.

I enjoyed writing about affirmations for beauty. A lot of black women have been told great lies that have made them blind to their beauty. My dear black woman, I urge you to embrace those beauty affirmations every day. I wrote it and dipped it in so much elegance just for you.

It takes courage for a black woman to walk towards empowerment and independence. I thought of this, and I poured my heart and soul into writing the chapters for courage, independence and empowerment. I bet you didn't notice this interconnection when you were reading this book. Does this make you smile? I hope it does. Black women are very pretty whenever they smile.

I wrote the chapter on leadership for every black woman in leadership. I am happy to see more black women go into leadership everyday. It is not easy being a black woman woman in leadership. It comes with a lot of troubles, stress and anxiety. But I believe in the beautiful power of the black woman to overcome them all. Also, I had this black women's leadership in mind when I wrote the stress management, anxiety and rest chapters. My dear black woman in leadership. You need these three to function optimally. Never turn them away no matter how busy you get. You need to be fit to be able to lead well. Don't you think so?

Black women love deeply and passionately. Some of them are very lucky in love. Others are not. For these ones, I wrote on healing and moving on. Then I wrote on self-love. My dear woman, you excel the most and love better when you love yourself first. That is why I am always of the opinion that you have no business trying to build a love relationship with someone if you do not love yourself first. Of course, there is no formula to loving. I wish you great love and happiness. But when it doesn't work out, I hope the healing affirmations help you move on. You'll definitely find the love that you desire.

Writing the last chapter of this book made me happy and sad at the same time. At first I was happy because I remembered black women I encountered in the past who wouldn't give up their originality for anything in the world. Originality is one of the greatest assets ever. I became sad at the thought of black women who have become strangers to their own selves by virtue of giving up on their trueness for various reasons. If you belong to this class of women, I hope you find yourself again. I hope you forgive yourself, and I hope that you always remember that nothing is worth your originality. You are perfect in all your flaws.

Now, I urge you to take action and create the kind of life that you have always wanted and dreamt of by employing what you have learnt in this book into your daily life. If you are unable to read this book as often as you desire, you could easily read the key points and get the needed value. My dear black woman, I truly enjoyed holding your hand through each affirmation. It was beautiful to reach you so closely like that. You are a gem.

I love you, dear black woman.

Thank you so much for listening

If you enjoyed this book would you consider leaving a review on Amazon?

For a small author and publisher like us, this is the only way to sell more copies from time to time, which is always nice.

Thank you again

EasyTube Zen Studio